POPULAR
MUSIC

The Popular Music Series

Popular Music, 1980–1989 is a revised cumulation of and supersedes Volumes 9 through 14 of the *Popular Music* series, all of which are still available:

Volume 9, 1980–84	Volume 12, 1987
Volume 10, 1985	Volume 13, 1988
Volume 11, 1986	Volume 14, 1989

Popular Music, 1920–1979 is also a revised cumulation of and supersedes Volumes 1 through 8 of the *Popular Music* series, of which Volumes 6 through 8 are still available:

Volume 1, 2nd ed., 1950–59	Volume 5, 1920–29
Volume 2, 1940–49	Volume 6, 1965–69
Volume 3, 1960–64	Volume 7, 1970–74
Volume 4, 1930–39	Volume 8, 1975–79

Popular Music, 1900–1919 is a companion volume to the revised cumulation.

This series continues with:

Volume 15, 1990	Volume 20, 1995
Volume 16, 1991	Volume 21, 1996
Volume 17, 1992	Volume 22, 1997
Volume 18, 1993	Volume 23, 1998
Volume 19, 1994	Volume 24, 1999

Other Books by Bruce Pollock

The Face of Rock and Roll: Images of a Generation

Hipper Than Our Kids?: A Rock and Roll Journal of the Baby Boom Generation

In Their Own Words: Popular Songwriting, 1955–1974

The Rock Song Index: The 7500 Most Important Songs of Rock and Roll

When Rock Was Young: The Heyday of Top 40

When the Music Mattered: Rock in the 1960s

ISSN 0886-442X

VOLUME 24

1999

POPULAR MUSIC

An Annotated Guide to American Popular Songs,
Including Introductory Essay, Lyricists and Composers Index,
Important Performances Index,
Awards Index, and List of Publishers

BRUCE POLLOCK
Editor

GALE GROUP

Detroit
New York
San Francisco
London
Boston
Woodbridge, CT

Bruce Pollock, *Editor*

Gale Group Staff

Jolen Marya Gedridge and Michael T. Reade, *Co-Editors*
Rita Runchock, *Managing Editor*

Dorothy Maki, *Manufacturing Manager*
Stacy Melson, *Buyer*

Cynthia Baldwin, *Production Design Manager*
Barbara J. Yarrow, *Graphic Services Supervisor*

Theresa Rocklin, *Director, Technical Support Services*
Charles Beaumont, *Senior Programmer/Analyst*

Library of Congress Catalog Card Number 85-653754
ISBN 0-7876-3311-9
ISSN 0886-442X

Printed in the United States of America

10 9 8 7 6 5 4 3 2 1

Contents

About the Book and How to Use It vii

Popular Music in 1999 xiii

Song Listings, A-Z 1

Lyricists & Composers Index 99

Important Performances Index 121

Awards Index 143

List of Publishers 145

About the Book
and How to Use It

This volume is the twenty-fourth of a series whose aim is to set down in permanent and practical form a selective, annotated list of the significant popular songs of our times. Other indexes of popular music have either dealt with special areas, such as jazz or theater and film music, or been concerned chiefly with songs that achieved a degree of popularity as measured by the music-business trade indicators, which vary widely in reliability.

Annual Publication Schedule

The first nine volumes in the *Popular Music* series covered sixty-five years of song history in increments of five or ten years. Volume 10 initiated a new annual publication schedule, making background information available as soon as possible after a song achieves prominence. Yearly publication also allows deeper coverage—approximately five hundred songs—with additional details about writers' inspiration, uses of songs, album appearances, and more.

Indexes Provide Additional Access

Three indexes make the valuable information in the song listings even more accessible to users. The Lyricists & Composers Index shows all the songs represented in *Popular Music, 1999,* that are credited to a given individual. The Important Performances Index tells at a glance which albums, musicals, films, television shows, or other media-featured songs are represented in the volume. The "Performer" category—first added to the index as "Vocalist" in the 1986 volume—allows the user to see with which songs an artist has been associated this year. The index is arranged by broad media category, then alphabetically by the show or album title, with the songs listed under each title. Finally, the Awards Index provides a list of the songs nominated for awards by the American Academy of

Motion Picture Arts and Sciences (Academy Award) and the American Academy of Recording Arts and Sciences (Grammy Award). Winning songs are indicated by asterisks.

List of Publishers

The List of Publishers is an alphabetically arranged directory providing addresses—when available—for the publishers of the songs represented in *Popular Music, 1999.* Also noted is the organization handling performance rights for the publisher—in the United States, the American Society of Composers, Authors, and Publishers (ASCAP) or Broadcast Music, Inc. (BMI); in Canada, the Society of Composers, Authors, and Music Publishers of Canada (SOCAN); and in Europe, the Society of European Songwriters and Composers (SESAC).

Tracking Down Information on Songs

Unfortunately, the basic records kept by the active participants in the music business are often casual, inaccurate, and transitory. There is no single source of comprehensive information about popular songs, and those sources that do exist do not publish complete material about even the musical works with which they are directly concerned. Four of the primary proprietors of basic information about our popular music are the major performing rights societies—ASCAP, BMI, SOCAN, and SESAC. Although each of these organizations has considerable information about the songs of its own writer and publisher members and has also issued indexes of its own songs, their files and published indexes are designed primarily for clearance identification by the commercial users of music. Their publications of annual or periodic lists of their "hits" necessarily include only a small fraction of their songs, and the facts given about these are also limited. ASCAP, BMI, SOCAN, and SESAC are, however, invaluable and indispensable sources of data about popular music. It is just that their data and special knowledge are not readily accessible to the researcher.

Another basic source of information about musical compositions and their creators and publishers is the Copyright Office of the Library of Congress. A computerized file lists each published, unpublished, republished, and renewed copyright of songs registered with the Office. It takes between six months and a year from the time of application before songs are officially registered (in some cases, songs have already been released before copyright registration begins). This file is helpful in determining the precise date of the declaration of the original ownership of musical works, but since some authors, composers, and publishers have been known to employ rather makeshift methods of protecting their works legally, there are songs listed in *Popular Music* that may not be found in the Library of Congress files.

Selection Criteria

In preparing the original volumes for this time period, the editor was faced with a number of separate problems. The first and most important of these was that of selection. The stated aim of the project—to offer the user as comprehensive and accurate a listing of significant popular songs as possible—has been the guiding criterion. The purpose has never been to offer a judgment on the quality of any songs or to indulge a prejudice for or against any type of popular music. Rather, it is the purpose of *Popular Music* to document those musical works that (1) achieved a substantial degree of popular acceptance, (2) were exposed to the public in especially notable circumstances, or (3) were accepted and given important performances by influential musical and dramatic artists.

Another problem was whether or not to classify the songs as to type. Most works of music are subject to any number of interpretations and, although it is possible to describe a particular performance, it is more difficult to give a musical composition a label applicable not only to its origin but to its subsequent musical history. In fact, the most significant versions of some songs are often quite at variance with their origins. Citations for such songs in *Popular Music* indicate the important facts about not only their origins but also their subsequent lives, rather than assigning an arbitrary and possibly misleading label.

Research Sources

The principal sources of information for the titles, authors, composers, publishers, and dates of copyright of the songs in this volume were the Copyright Office of the Library of Congress, ASCAP, BMI, SOCAN, SESAC, and individual writers and publishers. Data about best-selling recordings were obtained principally from three of the leading music business trade journals—*Billboard, Radio & Records,* and *Cash Box.* For the historical notes; information about foreign, folk, public domain, and classical origins; and identification of theatrical, film, and television introducers of songs, the editor relied upon collections of album notes, theater programs, sheet music, newspaper and magazine articles, and other material, both his own and that in the Lincoln Center Library for the Performing Arts in New York City.

About the Book and How to Use It

Contents of a Typical Entry

The primary listing for a song includes

- Title and alternate title(s)
- Country of origin (for non-U.S. songs)
- Author(s) and composer(s)
- Current publisher, copyright date
- Annotation on the song's origins or performance history

Title: The full title and alternate title or titles are given exactly as they appear on the Library of Congress copyright record or, in some cases, the sheet music. Since even a casual perusal of the book reveals considerable variation in spelling and punctuation, it should be noted that these are the colloquialisms of the music trade. The title of a given song as it appears in this series is, in almost all instances, the one under which it is legally registered.

Foreign Origin: If a song is of foreign origin, the primary listing indicates the country of origin after the title. Additional information may be noted, such as the original title, copyright date, writer, publisher in country of origin, or other facts about the adaptation.

Authorship: In all cases, the primary listing reports the author or authors and the composer or composers. The reader may find variations in the spelling of a songwriter's name. This results from the fact that some writers used different forms of their names at different times or in connection with different songs. In addition to this kind of variation in the spelling of writers' names, the reader will also notice that in some cases, where the writer is also the performer, the name as a writer may differ from the form of the name used as a performer.

Publisher: The current publisher is listed. Since *Popular Music* is designed as a practical reference work rather than an academic study, and since copyrights more than occasionally change hands, the current publisher is given instead of the original holder of the copyright. If a publisher has, for some reason, copyrighted a song more than once, the years of the significant copyright subsequent to the year of the original copyright are also listed after the publisher's name.

Annotation: The primary listing mentions significant details about the song's history—the musical, film, or other production in which the song was introduced or featured and, where important, by whom it was introduced, in the case of theater and film songs; any other performers identified with the song; first or best-selling recordings and album inclusions, indicating the performer and the record company; awards; and other relevant data. The name of a performer may be listed differently in connection with different songs, especially over a period of years. The name listed is the form of the name given in connection with a particular performance or record. Dates are provided for important recordings and performances.

Popular Music in 1999

Elliot Smith, it could have been you.

It was a scant couple of years ago, when the dour, reserved troubadour based in Brooklyn and signed to a tiny independent record label called Kill Rock Stars, operating out of Seattle, Washington, had his career-defining moment. Having already snagged the plum assignment of placing five songs into one of the year's most heralded films, *Good Will Hunting*, he must have greeted the news of the Oscar nomination of one of them, "Miss Misery," with a mixture of extreme pride and abject terror. Soon enough, the nervous, mumbling coffee house neophyte would be up there at the Shrine Auditorium performing in front of every anxious celebrity in the country as well as the hungry eyes of a nation. Up against Celine Dion's massive "My Heart Will Go On," from the unstoppable *Titanic*, a win in this category was already an impossibility, but a stunning bravura performance could well stem the very tide of hip hop and re-establish the lone singer-songwriter in a position of artistic prominence and relevance unheld since the heyday of the mellow 1970's. Instead, dwarfed by the venue, the magnitude of the challenge, even by his ill-fitting oversize tuxedo, Smith shrunk to the occasion, murmuring demurely in the face of that squall the all but tuneless, formless, and for all intents and purposes wordless tune. In three minutes it was thankfully over. The moment had passed.

Latin Breakout

This is what separates the men from the supermen, the mastery of moments. And so it was decreed that a year later another performer would get the same opportunity thrust into his lap at another high profile magnified event. When the former Menudo graduate Ricky Martin got his chance during the Grammy Awards to perform "La Copa De Vida (The Cup of Life)," during what might otherwise have been a commercial break inducing showcase of Latin music, the pressure and the discrepancies may have been less pronounced than they were with the overmatched Smith, but the result was nevertheless electrifying. Bringing everything he'd been working toward since he was a pre-teen prodigy to this extraordinary moment, Martin evoked the ghost of Elvis Presley's swiveling hips, in a three-minute marathon of joyous rhythm and sex. And in the aftermath of the cascading huzzahs, the spontaneous Rosie O'Donnell approbation, and what must have been the instant ricochets of ecstasy in households all throughout the world, Martin ascended on those clouds like a God, leading troops of deserving Latin and Latin-tinged artists as if on a mission through the padlocked doors of the Kingdom of Airplay and across America seemingly overnight and for the rest of the year.

Hunkered down over their half-empty coffee mugs, singer-songwriters meanwhile receded even deeper into their cups.

At the same time, the pop charts conferred their own praise on Martin ("Livin' La Vida Loca," "Shake Your Bon Bon," "She's All I Ever Had") and his brethren Marc Anthony ("I Need to Know") and Enrique Iglesias ("Bailamos"), his pseudo-brethren Lou Bega (whose "Mambo No. 5, a Little Bit of..." by way of Germany was at least based on the famed Tito Puente tune), and his sistren, the navel-baring actress Jennifer Lopez ("If You Had My Love"). Long-time Latin superstars benefited as well. Ruben Blades had a banner year ("Dia a Dia," "Vida"). The aforementioned Puente won a Grammy. The Buena Vista Social Club, led by Ibrahim Ferrer charmed fans and critics alike. But nobody hoisted the banner higher than Carlos Santana, whose album *Supernatural* not only put him in the rarefied Grammy company of Michael Jackson, Stevie Wonder, and Marvin Hamlisch, but effectively acted as both a tribute to his stunning twenty year career on the rock guitar boards and a testament to how well his music served an all-star lineup of young collaborators (Matchbox 20's Rob Thomas on the chart-dominating "Smooth," Everlast Schrody on the dark and moody "Put Your Lights On," and Dave Matthews on the lilting "Love of My Life").

Young Stars Emerge

The insistent rhythms of Latin music, based mainly in the hips, translated well to the otherwise teen-centric pop ears of 1999 radio. Not since the late 1980's, when Debbie Gibson, Tiffany, and the New Kids on the Block ruled the locker, stoop, and soda shoppe, had the teenage voice incurred such instant authenticity. As far as delivering tuneful lightweight anthems of teen love and adolescent anxiety, the prevailing credo seemed to be: Don't trust anyone over twenty—unless they were former members of the New Kids on the Block, two of whom effected semi-comebacks this year, Jordan Knight ("Give It to You") and Joey McIntyre ("I Love You Came Too Late").

Like tennis prodigies, and gymnastic waifs, the talented girls exploding out of the various high schools and performing arts academies into sudden fame, wealth, and cross-country touring commitments, were younger and younger this year and apt to be ferried from MTV to major commercial and movie tie-ins by more experienced svengalis with little thought to Debbie Gibsonesque longevity. Following the lead of Brandy ("Almost Doesn't Count"), who's already notched her initial squarely on Hollywood's Tree of Fame in TV's *Moesha* and *Cinderella*, and her similarly one-named compatriot Monica ("Angel of Mine"), 1999 saw the emergence of the peppy Britney Spears ("Sometimes"), the prim Christina Aquilera ("Genie in a Bottle," "What a Girl Wants"), the ethereal Charlotte Church ("Just Wave Hello"), and the effervescent Jessica Simpson ("I Wanna Love You Forever"). While most of these acts were essentially cut out of the pages of *Young Miss* (*Sassy* having gone down the tubes), their boy-group counterparts engendered quite a different reaction. When it came to the battle between the Backstreet Boys ("I Want It That Way," "Larger Than Life," "All I Have to Give"), 'N Sync ("God Must Have Spent a Little More Time on You") and 98 Degrees ("The Hardest Thing," "I Do Cherish You"), pop fans hadn't witnessed such intense factionalism since the Beach Boys, the Four Seasons, and the Association had it out in the 1960s. All in all, these harmony wars produced some of the most compelling singles since Dion & the Belmonts left the Bronx.

Urban Rhythms Still Strong

Not only that, for the first time in years, the realm of the hit single, previously the exclusive province of the rap and hip hop machine, was threatened by these voices of Suburbia, which provided a safe alternative to the endless supply of rhythmic novelties topped by random bursts of profanity that machine had been producing unmolested for much of the decade. Ever resilient, the forces of r&b righted themselves in time for a year of solid songwriting, toning down their various acts just a bit to accommodate the new purity of the approaching millennium, with infectious smashes like "Bills Bills Bills" by Destiny's Child, "Jamboree" by Naughty By Nature, "808" by Blaque, "Bling Bling" by B. G., featuring the ubiquitous likes of 'Lil Wayne and Juvenile, among others, "Get It on Tonite" by Montell Jordan, and "U Know What's Up" by Donell Jones.

Barry White completed a welcome comeback with "Staying Power." The Artist Formerly Known As the Artist Formerly Known As Prince (but now known just as The Artist) parlayed the inevitable revival of his classic "1999" with an invigorating new album, which spawned the hit "The Greatest Romance Ever Sold." And in a (very) belated effort to revamp his image, the estate of the late Tupac Shakur put out his remarkable take on the Bruce Hornsby classic "Changes." In the image makeover department, however, Robert Kelly led the way, emerging at century's end as the consummate writer, singer, producer, and nostalgia buff. The soulful sensitivity of "When a Woman's Fed Up" was a million enlightened miles from his early days of "Bump and Grind." And his bravura doo-wop inspired performance of "If I Could Turn Back Time" was a quantum leap past his previous two leaps of "I Believe I Can Fly" and "Gotham City."

Whitney Houston also leaped back into critical favor with the maturity of "It's Not Right But It's Okay" and the passion of "Heartbreak Hotel." Mary J. Blige polished her reputation as the reigning Queen of Soul with the Lauryn Hill-written and produced "All That I Can Say." Mariah Carey continued her hitmaking string with "Heartbreaker." Missy Elliott produced her share of gritty collaborations ("All N My Grill," with Big Boi and Nicole, and "Hot Boyz," with Nas, Eve, and Q-Tip). Some great new female voices emerged, like the Billie Holiday influenced Macy Gray ("I Try"), the commanding Kelis ("Caught out There") and the intense Me Shell NdegeOcello ("Satisfy"). But no females defined the year like the embattled trio, TLC. Possibly on the brink of breaking up, they nevertheless came together for a couple of the year's best songs, the poignant Tionne Watkins/Dallas Austin collaboration, "Unpretty," and the anthemic single girl call to arms, "No Scrubs," a lyric so defiant and threatening it immediately necessitated the male response "No Pigeons." Tionne even found time to include a song ("Tionne's Song") in her made for cassette audio-biography.

The biggest news in rap this year may have been the crossover success of the dirty white boy known as Eminem ("My Name Is"), but the more hopeful news was the critical and commercial breakthrough of the organization known as the Roots ("Silent Treatment," "You Got Me," with Erykah Badu). With deft wordplay attached to accomplished musical chops and a winning panoply of rogues and rhymers, like Rahzel (whose own "Southern Gul" was also accompanied by Badu), the Roots have by far performed the more deft crossover.

Greater Crossover Between Country, Rock, Folk, and Blues

At the other end of the musical spectrum, country music enjoyed perhaps its most creative year of the decade. Bolstered by the notion that lots of aging Baby Boomers were beginning to find in its wizened outlook and weathered repertoire a soft place to spend their post rock and roll years, the country sphere produced a series of quality special projects. Chief among them was an album done in tribute to the late Gram Parsons, the man who brought country music into rock in the 1960s, when he joined the Byrds. The lineup of contemporary artists covering his material was a tribute in itself: Wilco ("One Hundred Years from Now"), the Cowboy Junkies ("Ooh Las Vegas"), Lucinda Williams and David Crosby ("Return of the Grievous Angel"), Elvis Costello ("Sleepless Nights"), Chris Hillman and Steve Earle ("High Fashion Queen")—not only to his legacy but to the range of his enduring influence.

Steve Earle, proving himself in the last few years to be one of the most versatile and honest interpreters of rural American music, this year teamed up with the Del McCoury Band to offer another taste of his expansive and engaging vision ("Carrie Brown"). On the female side of bluegrass of course there's no one finer than Alison Krauss, who once again delivered the goods ("Forget About It"). Lately picking up credits as a country songwriter, the folk/poet John Prine offered a winsome and winning album of duets with some of the finest female voices in the business, highlighted by "Back Street Affair," with Patty Loveless, and "In Spite of Ourselves," with Iris Dement. Linda Ronstadt and Emmylou Harris gave us a duet album of their own, which included Jackson Browne's "For a Dancer" and Bruce Springsteen's "Across the Border." Then they did themselves one better, by coming out with the long await-ed *Trio II* with Dolly Parton (in which they revived Randy Newman's "Feels Like Home")—Newman himself released another album featuring some of his finest work ("I Miss You," "My Country").

Welcoming the songs of folk/pop and middle of the dirt road artists like Browne, Springsteen, and Newman into the country fold was a major move this year in widening country's creative berth. So was the recognition given to some peerless peers whose works may have fallen just a bit outside of contemporary country music's previously limited airspace. There was the long overdue Kinky Friedman anthology ("Marilyn and Joe"), new material by Guy Clark ("Red River"), posthumous gems from Townes Van Zandt ("To Live Is to Fly"), a career revival by George Jones ("Choices"), and a total career overhaul by Merle Haggard (his cover of Lefty Frizell's "That's the Way Love Goes" was a duet with pop neo-folkie Jewel). This new country constituency was the perfect audience as well for another nostalgia-soaked tribute, this one to the Greenwich Village of the 1960s, with contemporary singer-songwriters offering their interpretations of the era's classics. In it you could find Suzanne Vega and

John Cale doing Leonard Cohen's "So Long Marianne," Ron Sexsmith covering Tim Hardin's "Reason to Believe," the Richard & Mimi Farina gem "Pack up Your Sorrows" by Loudon Wainwright and Iris Dement, Irish rockers Black 47 re-invigorating Phil Ochs' "I Ain't Marchin' Anymore," among many others. Eric Andersen produced an album of new tunes (highlighted by the haunting "Rain Falls Down in Amsterdam"). A veritable fount of old timey music and wisdom, the Holy Modal Rounders, another wizened relic of the Greenwich Village era, also resurfaced to the great delight of connoisseurs everywhere ("The Tea Song").

While mainstream country music's weakest expansion move may have been the attempt to reinvent Garth Brooks as the rocker Chris Gaines ("Lost in You"), Dwight Yoakam more than proved his own rocking credibility with an album of covers (among them "Crazy Little Thing Called Love" from the Queen oeuvre). Mark Chesnutt knew a great song when he heard it ("I Don't Want to Miss a Thing"), even if it was originally introduced by the rock group Aerosmith. Kenny Chesney knew a great song title when he heard it ("You Had Me from Hello") even if it was introduced in the movie *Jerry McGuire*, which was written by former rock writer Cameron Crowe. Both LeAnn Rimes and Diamond Rio knew a great song writer when they heard one in Al Anderson ("Big Deal" and "Unbelievable," respectively), even if Al started out in life as a guitarist in the long-running rock and roll bar band NRBQ. And definitely Shania Twain knew a great producer when she married one, in Mutt Lange, who once reigned over the heavy metal arena when he worked with bands like Def Leppard. With his help, she continued to reign over country and pop audiences with "Come on Over," and "You've Got a Way," which benefited from its placement in the abjectly pop movie *Nottinghill*. Similarly, the Dixie Chicks didn't blink when offered a slot in *Runaway Bride* ("Ready to Run"). Of course, cover girl Faith Hill certainly knew what she was doing when she gave the okay for the use of "You Give Me Love" over the final credits of the final episode of TV's *Mad About You*. And the jovial and convivial Vince Gill wasn't about to say no to crooning a number written by lightweight popster Richard Marx ("If You Leave Me"), when it meant a chance to record with the ultimate diva Barbra Streisand. For all of these reasons and more, no one should have been amazed when Lonestar's "Amazed" crossed the mythical boundary between pop and country and became a major hit toward the end of the millennium. A lot of people were amazed, however, when NRBQ reunited (without Al Anderson) for yet another album of joyful bar band blues ("Pain").

Surely an honorary country bumpkin these days, for his choice of outfits at least, is Bob Dylan, who found his work popping up in the strangest places this year, mostly on TV. His duet with Joan Osborne on "Chimes of Freedom" was the showpiece of the otherwise dismal *The Sixties*, while B. B. King unearthed Bob's "Fur Slippers" which was far from the centerpiece of the equally dismal fifties tribute *Shake, Rattle & Roll* (that dubious honor belonged to the Leiber & Stoller chestnut "One Bad Stud," performed on the show by its star Brad Hawkins). Almost as odd a pairing occurred when punk rocker Mike Ness covered Dylan's "Don't Think Twice." Better luck was accorded Dylan influenced nasal apostles like Tom Petty ("Room at the Top," and "Free Girl Now," one of the first tunes by a major artist to be offered for free for a limited time over the Internet) and Loudon Wainwright ("Tonya's Twirls" and "You're Older Than You've Ever Been," which received wide exposure on national public television and radio). Neil Young reunited with his erstwhile buddies C,S&N, to give their album some much needed angst ("Out of Control," "Slowpoke" and the title tune, "Looking Forward"), while father of the year candidate David Crosby contributed the strident "Stand and Be Counted." Neo Beat icon Tom Waits came out with one of the best received albums of the year (and his career), with tunes as gruff and grizzly as any Merle Haggard could have sung, among them "What's He Building," "Hold On," "Big in Japan" and "House Where Nobody Lives." Bruce Springsteen buffed his performing legend with a massive reunion tour, topped off by a great new song ("The Promise"). Among the ranks of the newest New Dylans, Dan Bern remains in a class by himself (with the simply amazing Columbine inspired "Song for the Children" from a limited edition live album).

Elsewhere, the middle of the dirt road stretched across a particularly wide swath of Americana this year, taking us on journeys to visit some friends not heard from in decades, like Jesse Winchester ("That's What Makes You Strong"), Iggy Pop ("Shakin' All Over"), and Ronnie Spector ("Don't Worry Baby"). Cindy Bullens, once considered the great lost rock star of the 1970s, recovered from personal tragedy to produce the year's most inspiring effort ("Better Than I've Ever Been"). In some cases, the dirt road stretched all the way to England, where we found Van Morrison hard at work ("When the Leaves Come Falling Down"), David Bowie reinventing himself once again ("Thursday's Child"), the Eurythmics coming together once more, at least for an album ("17 Again"), the wonderful XTC temporarily getting it back together ("The Last Balloon") and Paul McCartney working through the loss of his beloved wife Linda by reviving his fondest childhood memories of rockabilly ("Blue Jean Bop").

But in this post-rock and roll universe, the genre that I first called middle of the dirt road over a decade ago, now encompasses more styles than ever, veering from folk and country and blues into sophisticated forms of jazz and pop as well (hip pop, if you will). The ascendance of jazz vocalist Diana Krall ("Popsicle Toes," "When I Look in Your Eyes") this year attests to the growing primacy of substantial music to satisfy the exceptional palates of an aging generation. Catering to this crowd you had Cassandra Wilson, with her tribute to Miles Davis ("Right Here, Right Now"), Abbey Lincoln ("Caged Bird"), Susannah McCorkle ("Laughing at Life," "Losing Hand," "Something to Live For"), Barbara Cook ("They Were You"), Betty Buckley ("New Ways to Dream," "Surrender").

Mixed Bag for Broadway Tunes

Broadway's favorite sister act, Alice Ripley and Emily Skinner, put out another album (featuring "What You Don't Know About Women," from *City of Angels* and "I'm Past My Prime" from *Lil Abner*). Some of Broadway's current leading ladies were featured on a new album, highlighted by Bebe Neuwirth and Karen Ziemba doing Kander & Ebb's "Nowadays." This year Barbra Streisand dusted off "Music That Makes Me Dance" again.

While classic Broadway tracks achieved surprising currency among many interpreters this year, the latest new shows to open on the once-Great White Way were less than dazzling. And the ones that may have had a chance to reach those heights generally closed before posterity could give them a helping hand, like Jason Robert Brown's *Parade* ("It's Not Over Yet") or Ricky Ian Gordon's *Dreams True* ("Space," "Finding Home"). Garnering some of the best reviews this year was Audra McDonald, for her performance in Robert John LaChuisa's operetta *Marie Christine* ("Way Back to Paradise"). Some of the worst reviews were generated by Frank Wildhorn's *The Civil War* ("Freedom's Child"). In between, *Kat and the Kings*, imported from South Africa, had a healthy run ("Cavala Kings") and *Hedwig and the Angry Inch* became a true cult favorite ("Angry Inch," "Tear Me Down"). While Elton John's *Aida* opened only on record ("Written in the Stars," "A Step Too Far," "Elaborate Lives") its slot on the schedule for 2000 bodes well for the year. As does the full-scale revival of the early Stephen Sondheim musical *Saturday Night*, this year showcased by the Pegasus Players ("Delighted I'm Sure," "I Remember That," "Exhibit A").

Films Remain a Fertile Field for Music

Not surprisingly, most songwriters still reserved their best tunes for the wide screen, where film directors have continued to hone their skills, not only as hitmakers and scene setters, but also as connoisseurs of the weird, the obscure, and the interesting cover song. While movies such as *Mystery Men* ("All Star"), *She's All That* ("Kiss Me"), *The Other Sister* ("Animal Song"), *Prince of Egypt* ("When You Believe"), and *Austin Powers: The Spy Who Shagged Me* ("Beautiful Stranger") all produced hit singles (with "When You Believe" snagging last year's Oscar for Best Song), it was *Rushmore*, *Magnolia* and *Man on the Moon* that grabbed all the critical publicity for superior song selection. In the *Rushmore* soundtrack devotees could find the British cult nugget from 1965, "Making Time," by Creation. In addition to songs by R.E.M. ("The Great Beyond"), whose "Man on the Moon" inspired the film about the late comedian Andy Kaufman in the first place, the real musical move was Jim Carrey's rendition of the kitsch classic "This Friendly World," first introduced in the movie *Hound Dog Man* by Fabian. And, showing just how often history has a way of repeating itself, especially in the music business, taking the Elliot Smith role this year as downtrodden singer songwriter, was Aimee Mann, who survived having her new album cancelled by a major label to place a slew of songs in the movie *Magnolia*, including eventual Oscar nominee "Save Me."

Hollywood also honored the fabulous fiends from *South Park* for their wittily off-color "Blame Canada" from the musical version of the devilish TV comedy. And where else but in Hollywood could you find such a range of inspired pairings as goth icon Marilyn Manson singing "Highway to Hell" (from *Detroit Rock City*), jazz princess Diana Krall crooning a Clint Eastwood tune "Why Should I Care" (from *True Crime*) and mainstream rocker Sheryl Crow offering her sedated take on the Guns 'N Roses epic "Sweet Child of Mine" (from *Big Daddy*). Presaging a Guns 'N Roses comeback in 2000, the band debuted a song called "Oh My God" in the film *End of Days*. *Teaching Mrs. Tingle* gave us a new version of Janis Ian's timeless plaint "At Seventeen" by Tara McLean.

Nevertheless, despite a double dip of Randy Newman ("When She Loved Me" sung by Sarah McLachlan in *Toy Story II* and "The Time of Your Life," written and sung by Newman in *A Bug's Life*), the biggest news in filmdom was the virtual monopoly held by Diane Warren over the hearts and minds of music directors everywhere. Warren placed prominent songs in no less than half a dozen major feature films this year, including *Runaway Bride* ("Blue Eyes Blue" by Eric Clapton), *Patch Adams* ("Faith of the Heart" by Rod Stewart), *Music of the Heart* ("Music of My Heart" by Gloria Estefan and 'N Sync), *Message in a Bottle* ("I Could Not Ask for More" by Edwin McCain), *The Other Sister* ("Loving You Is All I Know" by the Pretenders) and *Detroit Rock City* ("Nothing Can

Keep Me From You" by Kiss). In her spare time Ms. Warren also penned tunes for such high profile artists as Mariah Carey ("Can't Take That Away"), Trisha Yearwood ("I'll Still Love You More") and Whitney Houston ("I Learned from the Best"). Not a bad career for anyone else.

Bumpy Year for Alternative

With the emphasis decidedly on pop this year, rock and roll took a precipitous dip in hipness quotient, if not in great tunes. Alternative music, especially, on the cutting edge and rising five or six years ago, was commercially stagnant, except for the occasional appearance of a song on the soundtrack of *Dawson's Creek* or *Felicity*. Poster boy Beck came up with a bunch of new stuff ("Sexx Laws"), the prolific Robert Pollard of Guided By Voices ("Hold on Hope") was dutifully productive, as was Pavement, led by Stephen Malkmus ("Spit on a Stranger"), but they all spoke mainly to the converted. Lou Barlow and Sebadoh continued to pursue their lonely visions ("Weird"). Veteran scenestars, the Flaming Lips made a comeback ("Waitin' for a Superman") but there was no one waiting to greet them. Purists Pearl Jam had to resort to a cover song to get the biggest hit of their career ("Last Kiss"), while their Nirvana spin-off counterparts, the Foo Fighters fought a somewhat better fight with the catchy "Learn to Fly." Even last year's model alternative genre of Electronica faded from the general public's earshot, with only Fatboy Slim ("Praise You") and Moby ("Porcelain") producing significant new work. Last year's model alternative band, the Goo Goo Dolls continued to inhabit the Top 10, this year with the quiet "Black Balloon."

Nevertheless, The Dave Matthews Band was out there, jamming harder than ever ("Crush"). The Offspring ("Why Don't You Get a Job") were diligently wired into the belligerent attitude of the generation. Fountains of Wayne ("Troubled Times") and Robbie Williams ("Angels") were the year's critical favorites. And the New Radicals ("You Get What You Give") and Everlast ("What It's Like") contributed two of the year's best lyrics. But probably the best lyrics of the year were heard in Baz Luhrman's "Everybody's Free (to Wear Sunscreen)." These were the commencement comments written by Chicago columnist Mary Schmich a couple of years back but erroneously attributed to Kurt Vonnegut when they were widely disseminated over the Internet. They were then set to an existing melody, just in time for graduation 1999 (at Alternative schools everywhere).

Veteran Women Artists Lose Momentum

If 1998 was the Year of the Woman (Y1W), 1999 was Y2W, with many of the Lilith Fair veterans emerging or at least achieving their biggest fame in Y1W releasing generally disappointing follow up works, or coasting on their 1998 achievements, among them Jewel ("Down So Long"), Sarah McLachlan ("Angel," "I Will Remember You"), Beth Orton ("Stars All Seem to Weep"), and Ani DiFranco ("Jukebox," "Angel Food"). Tori Amos ("1000 Oceans") and Luscious Jackson ("Nervous Breakthrough") were still unable to fully exploit the potential of their early nineties debut albums. Shirley Manson's Garbage ("Special") were fairly inactive. By far the most exciting thing Melissa Ethridge ("Angels Would Fall") did this year was to announce the name of her child's father. On the other hand, Fiona Apple had the biggest Y2W breakthrough with a follow up album of her own, whose pretentious approximately 55 word title nearly obscured the fine material inside ("Paper Bag," "Fast as You Can," "I Know"). Susan Tedeschi ("Looking for Answers"), a Cambridge based blues-rock singer in the mold of Bonnie Raitt, got a surprise Grammy nomination for Best New Artist. And Beth Hart ("L.A. Song") made the year's most promising debut album aside from Macy Gray. Of course, the biggest year for a female was had by a veritable warhorse of the genre named Cher ("Believe"). But of all the contenders who else could actually play the role of Lilith in the movie?

Anyone who thinks that Meredith Brooks, another of last year's Y1W pretenders, defiled some sacred memories with her remake of Melanie's Woodstock tribute "Lay Down (Candles in the Rain)" was obviously distraught during the wholesale franchise destruction that accompanied this year's version of the aforementioned event. On a par with Ricky Martin shaking his bon bon with quintessential joie de vivre on national TV in February was the image of Limp Bizkit's Fred Durst urging his followers to "break things" in August as the festival grounds went up in flames.

Post-Grunge Rock Retains its Hard Edge

For delineating the historical yin and yang of rock versus pop this year you couldn't ask for a more distinct celebrity death match. While naysayers like our satirical old friend Mojo Nixon ("Rock and Roll Hall of Lame") and the morbidly inclined thespian Marilyn Manson ("Rock Is Dead") took the low road, others like Kid Rock ("Cowboy," "Bawitda-ba"), Sugar Ray ("Someday," "Every Morning"), Korn ("Falling Away from Me"), Blink 182 ("What's My Age Again," "All the Small Things"), the incendiary Limp Bizkit ("Nookie," "Re-arranged"), the

Red Hot Chili Peppers ("Scar Tissue") Chris Cornell ("Can't Change Me") and Metallica ("No Leaf Clover") seemed instead to be sincere in their intent to restore at least a semblance of danger to the once macho art of headbanging.

To the danger, people like Zack De La Rocha of Rage Against the Machine ("Born of a Broken Man," "Guerrilla Radio") and Trent Reznor of Nine Inch Nails ("The Day the World Went Away," "We're in This Together") were attempting to add a touch of the artist.

Deep in its underground hovel as the new century dawns, I believe the beast of rock still breathes.

Bruce Pollock
Editor

A

Across the Border
Words and music by Bruce Springsteen.
Bruce Springsteen Publishing, 1999.
Introduced by Linda Ronstadt and Emmylou Harris with Neil Young in
the album *Western Wall The Tucson Sessions* (Asylum, 99).

All I Have to Give
Words and music by Full Force.
P-Blast Music, 1999/Zomba Music, 1999.
Best-selling record by the Backstreet Boys in the album *Millennium*
(Jive, 99).

All N My Grill
Words and music by Missy Elliott, Tim Mosley, and A. Patton.
Mass Confusion Music, 1999/Virginia Beach Music, 1999/WB Music,
1999/Gnat Booty Music, 1999/Chrysalis Music Group, 1999.
Best-selling record by Missy "Misdemeanor" Elliott featuring Big Boi
and Nicole in the album *Da Real World* (The Gold Mind/East West,
99).

All Night Long
Words and music by Faith Evans, Ron Lawrence, Sean Combs, Schon
Crawford, Todd Russaw, Todd Gaither, Galen Underwood, and
Bertram Reed.
Chyna Baby Music, 1999/Janice Combs Music, 1999/EMI-Blackwood
Music Inc., 1999/Ausar Music, 1999/BMG Music, 1999/Justin Combs
Music, 1999/EMI-April Music, 1999/Brother 4 Brothers, 1999.
Best-selling record by Faith Evans featuring Puff Daddy in the album
Keep the Faith (Bad Boy, 99).

All the Small Things
Words and music by Tom Delong and Mark Hoppus.
EMI-April Music, 1999/Fun with Goats Music, 1999.
Best-selling record by Blink 182 in the album *Enema of the State*
(MCA, 99).

All Star
Words and music by Gregory Camp.
Warner-Tamerlane Music, 1999/Squish Moth Music, 1999.
Best-selling record by Smash Mouth in the album *Astro Lounge* (Interscope, 99). From the film *Mystery Men*.

All That I Can Say
Words and music by Lauryn Hill.
Sony ATV Music, 1999/Obverse Creation Music, 1999.
Best-selling record by Mary J. Blige in the album *Mary* (MCA, 99) .Nominated for a Grammy Award, Best R&B Song of the Year, 1999.

All Things Considered
Warner-Tamerlane Music, 1999/Smith Haven Music, 1999.
Best-selling record by Yankee Grey in the album *Untamed* (Monument, 99).

All the Wasted Time
Words and music by Jason Robert Brown.
Revived by the Original Cast featuring Brent Carver and Carolee Carmello in the album *Parade* (RCA, 99)

All the Way
Words and music by Robert Cray and Turner.
Robert Cray Music, 1999.
Introduced by Robert Cray in the album *Take Your Shoes Off* (Rykodisc, 99).

Almost Doesn't Count
Words and music by Shelly Peiken and Guy Roche.
Sushi Too Music, 1999/Hidden Pun Music, 1999/Warner-Tamerlane Music, 1999/Manuiti LA Music, 1999.
Best-selling record by Brandy in the album *Never Say Never* (Atlantic, 99).

Almost Home
Words and music by Mary Chapin Carpenter, Annie Roboff, and Beth Neilsen Chapman.
Why Walk, 1999/Almo Music Corp., 1999/BNC, 1999/Anwa Music, 1999.
Best-selling record by Mary Chapin Carpenter in the album *Party Doll and Other Favorites* (Columbia, 99).

Amazed
Words and music by Marv Green, Aimee Mayo, and Chris Lindsay.
Warner-Tamerlane Music, 1999/Golden Wheat Music, 1999/Careers-BMG Music, 1999/Silverkiss Music, 1999/Dreamworks, 1999/Songs of Nashville, 1999/Cherry River Music Co., 1999.
Best-selling record by Lonestar in the album *Lonely Grill* (BNA, 99)

.Nominated for a Grammy Award, Best Country Song of the Year, 1999.

American Woman (Canadian)
Words and music by Burton Cummings, M. J. Kale, Garry Peterson, and Randy Bachman.
Shillelagh Music, 1970.
Best-selling record by Lenny Kravitz in the film and soundtrack album *Austin Powers: The Spy Who Shagged Me* (Maverick/Virgin, 99).

Angel (Canadian)
Words and music by Sarah McLachlan and Pierre Marchand.
Sony ATV Songs, 1998/Tyde, 1998/Studio Nomado Music, 1998.
Best-selling record by Sarah McLachlan in the album *Mirror Ball* (Arista, 98).

Angel Food
Words and music by Ani DiFranco.
Righteous Babe Music, Buffalo, 1999.
Introduced by Ani DiFranco in the album *Up Up Up Up Up Up* (Righteous Babe, 99).

Angels (English)
Words and music by Robbie Williams.
EMI-Blackwood Music Inc., 1999/BMG Music, 1999.
Introduced by Robbie Williams in the album *Millennium* (Capital, 99).

Angels Would Fall
Words and music by Melissa Etheridge and John Shanks.
MLE Music, 1999/Almo Music Corp., 1999/Virgin Music, 1999/Line On Music, 1999.
Best-selling record by Melissa Ethridge in the album *Breakdown* (Island, 99).Nominated for a Grammy Award, Best Rock Song of the Year, 1999.

Angry Inch
Words and music by Stephen Trask.
So Do My Songs, 1998.
Revived by John Cameron Mitchell in the original cast album *Hedwig and the Angry Inch* (Atlantic, 99).

The Animal Song (Australian)
Words and music by Darron Hayes and Daniel Jones.
Rough Cut Music, 1999.
Best-selling record by Savage Garden in the film and soundtrack album *The Other Sister* (Hollywood/Columbia, 98).

Ann Don't Cry
Words and music by Stephen Malkmus.

Treble Kicker Music, 1999.
Introduced by Pavement in the album *Terror Twilight* (Matador, 99).

Another Sinner's Prayer
Words and music by Jim Lauderdale.
Laudersongs, 1999.
Introduced by Jim Lauderdale and Ralph Stanley in the album *I Feel Like Singing Today* (Rebel, 99).

Anyone Else
Words and music by Radney Foster.
Shobi Music, 1998/St. Julien Music, 1998.
Best-selling record by Collin Raye in the album *Walls Come Down* (Epic, 98).

Anything But Down
Words and music by Sheryl Crow.
Old Crow, Los Angeles, 1999/Warner-Tamerlane Music, 1999.
Best-selling record by Sheryl Crow in the album *The Globe Sessions* (A&M, 99).

Anywhere
Words and music by Daron Jones, Michael Keith, Quinnes Parker, Jason Boyd, Jr., Marvin Scandrick, Lamont Maxwell, and Zane Copeland.
Kalinmia, 1999/Justin Combs Music, 1999/EMI-April Music, 1999.
Best-selling record by 112 featuring Lil 'Z in the album *Room 112* (Bad Boy/Arista, 99).

Around the World
Words and music by Anthony Keidis, John Frusciante, Chad Smith, and Flea (pseudonym for Michael Balzary).
Moebetoblame Music, 1999.
Best-selling record by Red Hot Chili Peppers in the album *Californication* (Warner Brothers, 99).

At My Most Beautiful
Words and music by Michael Stipe, Mike Mills, and Peter Buck.
Temporary Music, 1998/Warner-Tamerlane Music, 1999.
Introduced by R.E.M. in the album *Up* (Warner Brothers, 98).

At Seventeen
Words and music by Janis Ian.
Aspen Fair Music, 1975.
Revived by Tara McLean in the film and soundtrack album *Teaching Mrs. Tingle* (Capitol, 99).

B

Baby Can I Hold You
Words and music by Tracy Chapman.
EMI-April Music, 1988.
Revived by Boyzone in the album *Where We Belong* (Polygram, 99).

Baby Love
Words and music by Joan Osborne, Jack Petruzelli, Rainy Orteca, and
　Erik Penna.
Womanly Hips Music, 1999/Jacksnacks Music, 1999/Groin Pull Music,
　1999/Sleez Tak Music, 1999.
Introduced by Joan Osborne in the film and soundtrack album *For the
　Love of the Game* (MCA, 99).

Back at One
Words and music by Brian McKnight.
Cancelled Lunch Music, 1999/Shobi Music, 1999.
Best-selling record by Brian McKnight in the album *Back at One*
　(Motown, 99). Revived by Mark Wills in the album *Permanently*
　(Polygram, 2000).

Back Street Affair
Words and music by John Prine.
Weowna Music, 1999.
Introduced by John Prine and Patty Loveless in the album *In Spite of
　Ourselves* (Oh Boy, 99).

Back That Thang Up
Words and music by Juvenile (pseudonym for Terius Gray), Mannie
　Fresh, and Lil Wayne.
Money Mack Music, 1999.
Best-selling record by Juvenile featuring Mannie Fresh and Lil Wayne
　in the album *400 Degreez* (Cash Money/Universal, 99).

Back 2 Good
Words and music by Rob Thomas and Matt Serletic.

5

EMI-Blackwood Music Inc., 1996/Bidnis Inc Music, 1996/Melusic Music, 1996.

Revived by Matchbox 20 in the album *Live from Australia* (Lava/Atlantic, 99).

Bailamos (English)

Words and music by Paul Barry and Mark Taylor.

Rive Droite Music, 1999.

Best-selling record by Enrique Iglesias in the film and soundtrack album *Wild Wild West* (Overbrook/Interscope, 99).

Battle Flag

Words and music by Steve Fisk, Shawn Smith, and Prince (pseudonym for Prince Rogers Nelson).

Quality First Music, 1999/WB Music, 1999.

Best-selling record by the Lo Fidelity All Stars in the album *How to Operate with a Blown Mind* (Skint/Sub Pop, 99).

Bawitdaba

Words and music by Robert Ritchie, Eric Shafer, James Trombly, and John Travis.

Thirtytwo Mile Music, 1999/Squamosal Music, 1999/Raje Music, 1999/Cradle the Balls Music, 1999/Warner-Tamerlane Music, 1999.

Best-selling record by Kid Rock in the album *Devil Without a Cause* (Top Dog/Lava/Atlantic, 99).

Beautiful Stranger (American-English)

Words and music by Madonna (pseudonym for Madonna Louise Veronica Ciccone) and William Orbit.

WB Music, 1999/Twentieth Century-Fox Music Corp., 1999/Rondor Music Inc., 1999/Almo Music Corp., 1999.

Best-selling record by Madonna in the film and soundtrack album *Austin Powers: The Spy Who Shagged Me* (Maverick, 99).Won a Grammy Award for Best Song Written for a Movie 1999.

Beautiful View (English)

Words and music by Ron Sexsmith.

Studio Nomado Music, 1999/Warner-Tamerlane Music, 1999.

Introduced by Ron Sexsmith in the album *Whereabouts* (Interscope, 99).

Believe (English)

Words and music by Brian Higgins, Stuart McLennan, Walter Collins, Steve Torch, Timothy Powell, Matthew Gray, and Paul Barry.

Right Bank Music, 1998/WB Music, 1999.

Best-selling record by Cher in the album *Believe* (Warner Brothers, 98) .Nominated for a Grammy Award, Best Record of the Year, 1999.

The Best for You

Words and music by Ricky Ian Gordon and Tina Landau.

Introduced by Jeff McCarthy and Judy Kuhn in the musical *Dreams True*.

Better Days (and the Bottom Drops Out)
Words and music by Matt Sims and Dave Cooley.
WB Music, 1999/Civis Rex Music, 1999.
Best-selling record by Citizen King in the album *Mobile Estates* (Warner Brothers, 99).

Better Than I've Ever Been
Words and music by Cindy Bullens.
Mammy's Geetar Music, 1999.
Introduced by Cindy Bullens in the album *Somewhere Between Heaven and Earth* (Blue Lobster/Artemis, 99).

Big Deal
Words and music by Al Anderson and Jeffrey Steele.
Al Andersongs, Nashville, 1999/Mighty Nice Music, 1999/Bluewater, 1999/Windswept Pacific, 1999/Yellow Desert Music, 1999/My Life's Work Music, 1999.
Best-selling record by LeAnn Rimes in the album *LeAnn Rimes* (Curb, 99).

Big in Japan
Words and music by Tom Waits.
Jalma Music, 1999.
Introduced by Tom Waits in the album *Mule Variations* (Epitaph, 99).

Bills Bills Bills
Words and music by Kandi Burruss, LeToya Luckett, Beyonce Knowles, Kevin Briggs, and Kelendria Rowland.
Shek' Em Down Music, 1999/Hitco Music, 1999/Kandacy Music, 1999/Jimi-Lane Music, 1999/EMI-April Music, 1999/Beyonce Music, 1999/Le Tonya Music, 1999/Kelendria Music, 1999.
Best-selling record by Destiny's Child in the album *The Writing's on the Wall* (Columbia, 99).Nominated for a Grammy Award, Best R&B Song of the Year, 1999.

Black Balloon
Words and music by Johnny Rzeznik.
Corner of Clark and Kent, 1998/Virgin Music, 1998.
Best-selling record by Goo Goo Dolls in the album *Dizzy Up the Girl* (Warner Brothers, 98).

Blame Canada
Words and music by Trey Parker and Marc Shaiman.
Introduced by the voices of Mary Kay Bergman (as Sheila Broflovski, Liane Cartman, Sharon Marsh, and Mrs. McCormick) in the film and

soundtrack album *South Park: Bigger, Longer & Uncut* (Atlantic, 99) .Nominated for an Academy Award, Best Song of the Year, 1999.

Bling Bling

Words and music by Mannie Fresh, Lil Wayne, and Baby.
Money Mack Music, 1999.
Best-selling record by B. G., featuring Baby, Turk, Mannie Fresh, Juvenile & Lil Wayne in the album *Chopper City in the Ghetto* (Cash Money/Universal, 99).

Bliss

Words and music by Tori Amos.
Sword and Stone Music, 1999.
Best-selling record by Tori Amos in the album *To Venus and Back* (Atlantic, 99).

Blue (Da Ba Dee) (Italian)

English words and music by Maurizio Lobina, Randone, and Massimo Gabutti.
Copyright Control, 1999.
Best-selling record by Eiffel 65 in the album *Europop* (Republic/ Universal, 99).

Blue Eyes Blue

Words and music by Diane Warren.
Realsongs, 1999.
Best-selling record by Eric Clapton in the film and soundtrack album *Runaway Bride* (Reprise, 99).

Blue Jean Bop

Words and music by Hal Levy and Gene Vincent.
Morley Music Co., Inc., 1957.
Revived by Paul McCartney in the album *Run Devil Run* (Capitol, 99).

Blue Monday (English)

Words and music by Bernard Sumner, Gillian Gilbert, Peter Hook, and Steven Morris.
WB Music, 1982/Be Music, 1982.
Revived by Orgy in the album *Candy Ass* (Elementree/Reprise, 99).

Boom Boom

Words and music by Cy Coleman and Carolyn Leigh.
Edwin H. Morris, 1962.
Revived by Martin Short in the musical *Little Me* .

Born of a Broken Man

Words and music by Zack De La Rocha, Timothy Commerford, Tom Morello, and Brad Wilk.
Retribution Music, 1999/Sony ATV Songs, 1999.

Introduced by Rage Against the Machine in the album *The Battle of Los Angeles* (Epic, 99).

The Boys Are Back in Town (Irish)
Words and music by Phil Lynott.
R.S.O. Publishing Inc., 1976.
Revived by Everclear in the film and soundtrack album *Detroit Rock City* (Polygram, 99).

Breathe
Words and music by Holly Lamar and Stephanie Bentley.
Caliv Music, 1999/Shobi Music, 1999/Hope Chest Music, 1999.
Best-selling record by Faith Hill in the album *Breathe* (Warner Brothers Nashville, 99).

Bring It All to Me
Words and music by B. K. Lawrence, Corey Rooney, L Ruby, L. Lewis, K. Spencer, W. Shelby, N. Sylvers, and L. Van Horsen.
B.K. Lawrence Music, 1999/Warner-Tamerlane Music, 1999/Cori Tiffani Music, 1999/Sony ATV Songs, 1999/Mawkeens Music, 1999/ Sony ATV Music, 1999.
Best-selling record by Blaque in the album *Blaque* (Track Masters/ Columbia, 99).

Buffy the Vampire Slayer
Words and music by Charles Dennis, Parry Gripp, and Stephen Sherlock.
TCF Music, 1999.
Introduced by Nerf Herder in the TV Show and on the soundtrack album *Buffy the Vampire Slayer* (TVT Soundtrax, 99).

Bug a Boo
Words and music by Kevin Briggs, Kandi Burruss, Beyonce Knowles, LeToya Luckett, Latavia Robertson, and Kelendria Rowland.
Hitco Music, 1999/Shek' Em Down Music, 1999/Windswept Pacific, 1999/Kandacy Music, 1999/Jimi-Lane Music, 1999/EMI-April Music, 1999/Beyonce Music, 1999/Le Tonya Music, 1999.
Best-selling record by Destiny's Child in the album *The Writing's on the Wall* (Columbia, 99).

Burn to Shine
Words and music by Ben Harper.
Virgin Music, 1999/Innocent Criminal, 1999.
Introduced by Ben Harper and the Innocent Criminals in the album *Burn to Shine* (Virgin, 99).

C

Caged Bird
Words and music by Abbey Lincoln.
Moseka Music, 1999.
Introduced by Abbey Lincoln in the album *Wholly Earth* (Verve, 99).

Calling My Baby Back
Words and music by Lina Koutrakous and Mark Hartman.
Plyner Music, 1999.
Introduced by Lina Koutrakos (WKF, 99).

Can't Change Me
Words and music by Chris Cornell.
You Make Me Sick, I Make Music, 1999.
Best-selling record by Chris Cornell in the album *Euphoria Morning*
   A&M/Interscope, 99).

Can't Find My Way Home
Words and music by Stevie Winwood.
Warner-Tamerlane Music, 1999.
Revived by Alana Davis in the film and soundtrack album *Mod Squad*
   (Elektra, 99).

Can't Stand It
Words and music by Jeff Tweedy, Jay Bennett, John Stirratt, and Ken
   Coomer.
Words Ampersand Music, 1999/Warner-Tamerlane Music, 1999/You
   Want a Piece of This Music, 1999/George M. Cohan Music
   Publishing Co., 1999/Poeyfarre Music, 1999/Ft. Toe Music, 1999.
Introduced by Wilco in the album *Summer Teeth* (Reprise, 99).

Can't Take That Away (Mariah's Theme)
Words and music by Mariah Carey and Diane Warren.
Realsongs, 1999/Rye Songs, 1999/Sony ATV Songs, 1999.
Introduced by Mariah Carey in the album *Rainbow* (Columbia, 99).

Carrie Brown
Words and music by Steve Earle.
WB Music, 1999.
Introduced by Steve Earle and the Del McCoury Band in the album *The Mountain* (K-Squared, 99).

Cathedral Heat
Words and music by Kristin Hersh.
Yes Dear, 1999.
Introduced by Kristin Hersh in the album *Sky Motel* (4AD, 99).

Caught out There
Words and music by Chad Hugo, Pharrell Williams, and Kelis.
The Waters of Nazareth Music, 1999/EMI-April Music, 1999/EMI-Blackwood Music Inc., 1999/Chase Chad Music, 1999.
Introduced by Kelis in the album *Kaleidoscope* (Virgin, 99).

Cavala Kings
Words and music by David Kramer and Taliep Peterson.
Plyner Music, 1999.
Introduced by Cast in the musical and original cast album *Kat and the Kings* (Relativity, 99).

Central Reservation (Canadian)
Words and music by Beth Orton.
EMI-Blackwood Music Inc., 1999.
Introduced by Beth Orton in the album *Central Reservation* (DeConstruction/Arista, 99).

C'est La Vie (Irish)
Words and music by Lindsay Arnaou, Ray Hedges, Martin Brannigan, Tracey Ackerman, Edele Lynch, Keavy Lynch, and Sinead O'Connor.
Sugar Free Music, 1999/Bucks Music, 1999/19 Music, 1999/Chrysalis Music Group, 1999/BMG Music, 1999/Polygram Music Publishing Inc., 1999.
Best-selling record by B*Witched in the album *B*Witched* (Epic, 99).

Changes
Words and music by Tupac Shakur and Bruce Hornsby.
Josma's Dream Music, 1999/Universal Music Corp., 1999/Basically Zappo Music, 1999/WB Music.
Best-selling record by 2Pac in the album *Best Of* (Amaru/Death Row/Interscope, 98).

Chante's Got a Man
Words and music by James Harris, III, Terry Lewis, Chante Moore, and George Jackson.
Flyte Tyme Tunes, 1999/EMI-April Music, 1999/EMI-Blackwood Music Inc., 1999/Screen Gems-EMI Music Inc., 1999/Chante 7 Music, 1999.

Best-selling record by Chante Moore in the album *This Moment Is Mine* (Silas/MCA, 99).

The Chemicals Between Us
Words and music by Gavin Rossdale.
Mad Dog Winston Music, 1999/Ensign Music, 1999.
Best-selling record by Bush in the album *Science of Things* (Trauma, 99).

Chimes of Freedom
Words and music by Bob Dylan (pseudonym for Robert Allen Zimmerman).
Special Rider Music, 1964.
Revived by Bob Dylan and Joan Osborne in the TV show and soundtrack album *The Sixties* (Mercury, 99).

Choices
Words and music by Mike Curtis and Billy Yates.
Boondocks Music, 1997/Mack Loyd Wadkins Music, 1997.
Best-selling record by George Jones in the album *Cold Hard Truth* (Asylum, 99).Nominated for a Grammy Award, Best Country Song of the Year, 1999.

Climb to Safety
Words and music by Jerry Joseph and Glenn Esparza.
RTP Music, 1999.
Introduced by Widespread Panic in the album *Til the Medicine Takes* (Capricorn, 99).

Come on up to the House
Words and music by Tom Waits.
Jalma Music, 1999.
Introduced by Tom Waits in the album *Mule Variations* (Epitaph, 99).

Come on Over
Words and music by Shania Twain and Robert John Lange.
Songs of Polygram, 1999/Zomba Music, 1999/Loon Echo Music, 1999.
Best-selling record by Shania Twain in the album *Come on Over* (Mercury, 99).Won a Grammy Award for Best Country Song of the Year 1999.

Conversation on a Barstool (Irish)
Words and music by Bono (pseudonym for Paul Hewson) and Edge (pseudonym for Dave Evans).
Songs of Polygram, 1996.
Revived by Marianne Faithfull in the album *A Perfect Stranger* (Chronicles/Island, 99).

Cowboy
Words and music by Robert Ritchie, Eric Shafer, James Trombly, and John Travis.
Thirtytwo Mile Music, 1999/Squamosal Music, 1999/Raje Music, 1999/ Cradle the Balls Music, 1999/Warner-Tamerlane Music, 1999.
Best-selling record by Kid Rock in the album *Devil Without a Cause* (Top Dog/Lava/Atlantic, 99).

Crawl Back (under My Stone) (English)
Words and music by Richard Thompson.
Bug Music, 1999.
Introduced by Richard Thompson in the album *Mock Tudor* (Capitol, 99).

Crazy Little Thing Called Love (English)
Words and music by Freddie Mercury.
Queen Music Ltd., 1981/Beechwood Music, 1999.
Best-selling record by Dwight Yoakam in the album *Last Chance for a Thousand Years* (Reprise Nashville, 99).

Crush
Words and music by Dave Matthews.
Colden Grey Music, New York, 1999.
Best-selling record by Dave Matthews Band in the album *Before These Crowded Streets* (RCA, 98).

D

David Duchovny
Words and music by Bree Sharp and Simon Austin.
Warner-Tamerlane Music, 1999.
Introduced by Bree Sharp in the album *A Cheap and Evil Girl* (Trauma, 99).

The Day the World Went Away
Words and music by Trent Reznor.
TVT, NYC, 1999/Leaving Hope Music, 1999.
Best-selling record by Nine Inch Nails in the album *The Fragile* (Nothing/Interscope, 99).

Delighted I'm Sure
Words and music by Stephen Sondheim.
Burthen Music Co., Inc., 1954.
Revived by the Pegasus Players in the musical *Saturday Night*.

Dia a Dia (Every Day)
Words and music by Ruben Blades.
Ruben Blades Music, 1999.
Introduced by Ruben Blades in the album *Tiempas* (Sony Discos, 99).

Did You Ever Know
Words and music by Peabo Bryson.
PB Music, 1999.
Introduced by Peabo Bryson in the album *Unconditional Love* (Private, 99).

Did You Ever Think
Words and music by Robert Kelly, Curtis Mayfield, Jean Claude Olivier, and Samuel Barnes.
Zomba Music, 1999/R. Kelly Music, 1999/Warner-Tamerlane Music, 1999/Twelve & Under Music, 1999/Slam U Well Music, 1999/Camad Music, Inc., 1999.
Best-selling record by R. Kelly in the album *R.* (Jive, 99).

Dizzy Duck
Words and music by John Trudell.
Poet Tree Music, 1999/Blackhawk Music Co., 1999.
Introduced by John Trudell in the album *Blue Indians* (Dangerous/
    Inside, 99).

The Dolphin's Cry
Words and music by Ed Kowalczyk.
Loco De Amor, New York, 1999/Audible Sun, New York, 1999.
Best-selling record by Live in the album *The Distance to Here*
    (Radioactive/MCA, 99).

Don't Come Crying to Me
Words and music by Vince Gill and Reid Nelsen.
Englishtown Music, 1999/Vinny Mae Music, 1999.
Best-selling record by Vince Gill in the album *The Key* (MCA, 99).

Don't Make Promises
Words and music by Tim Hardin.
Fort Knox Music Co., 1966/Trio Music Co., Inc., 1966/Allen Stanton
    Productions, 1966.
Revived by Chris Smither in the album *Drive You Home Again* (High
    Tone, 99).

Don't Think Twice
Words and music by Bob Dylan (pseudonym for Robert Allen
    Zimmerman).
Special Rider Music, 1963.
Revived by Mike Ness in the album *Cheating at Solitaire* (Time Bomb,
    99).

Don't Worry
Words and music by Marty Robbins.
Elvis Presley Music, 1960/Unichappell Music Inc., 1960.
Revived by LeAnn Rimes in the album *LeAnn Rimes* (Curb, 99).

Don't Worry Baby
Words and music by Brian Wilson and Roger Christian.
Irving Music Inc., 1964.
Revived by Ronnie Spector in the album *She Talks to Rainbows* (Kill
    Rock Stars, 99).

Down
Words and music by Dean Deleo and Scott Weiland.
Virgin Music, 1999.
Best-selling record by Stone Temple Pilots in the album *#4* (Atlantic,
    99).

Down on the Corner
Words and music by John Fogerty.
Jondora Music, 1969.
Revived by the Mavericks in the TV Show and soundtrack album *King of the Hill* (Elektra, 99).

Down So Long
Words and music by Jewel Kilcher.
WB Music, 1999, 1999/Wiggly Tooth Music.
Best-selling record by Jewel in the album *Spirit* (Atlantic, 99).

Dragway 42 (English)
Words and music by Chrissie Hynde.
Jerk Awake Music, Los Angeles, 1999.
Introduced by the Pretenders in the album *Viva El Amor* (Warner Brothers, 99).

Drive Me Wild
Words and music by Mark A. Miller, Gregg Hubbard, and Mike Lawler.
Cootermo Music, Nashville, 1999/Traveling Zoo, 1999/Myrt & Chuck's Boy Music, 1999/Caliv Music, 1999.
Best-selling record by Sawyer Brown in the album *Drive Me Wild* (Curb, 99).

Drivin' Nails in My Coffin
Words and music by Jerry Irby.
Anne-Rachel Music Corp., 1947.
Revived by Willie Nelson and Beck in the film and soundtrack album *Hi Lo Country* (TVT Soundtrax, 99).

E

Echo
Words and music by Kristin Hersh.
Yes Dear, 1999.
Introduced by Kristin Hersh in the album *Sky Motel* (4AD, 99).

808
Words and music by Robert Kelly and Natina Reed.
R. Kelly Music, 1999/Dotted Line Music, 1999.
Best-selling record by Blaque in the album *Blaque* (Track Masters/
  Columbia, 99).

Elaborate Lives (English)
Words and music by Elton John and Tim Rice.
Happenstance Music, 1999/Sixty Four Square Music, 1999/Wonderland
  Music, 1999.
Introduced by Heather Headley in the album *Elton John's Aida* (Rocket/
  Island, 99).

Empty Hearts
Words and music by Michael McDonald and Michael Johnson.
Genevieve Music, 1999/World Song Publishing, Inc., 1999.
Revived by Alison Krauss in the album *Forget About It* (Rounder, 99).

Enemy
Words and music by Travis Meeks.
Scrogrow Music, 1999/Warner-Tamerlane Music, 1999.
Best-selling record by Days of the New in the album *Days of the New*
  (Outpost/Universal, 99).

Everest
Words and music by Ani DiFranco.
Righteous Babe Music, Buffalo, 1999.
Introduced by Ani Difranco in the album *Up Up Up Up Up Up*
  (Righteous Babe, 99).

Every Morning
Words and music by Mark McGrath, David Kahne, Richard Bean, Abel Zarate, Pablo Tellez, Craig Bullock, Charles Farrier, Joseph Nichol, and Rodney Sheppard.
E Equals Music, 1999/Warner-Chappell Music, 1999/See Squared Music, 1999/Grave Lack of Talent Music, 1999/WB Music, 1999/Canteberry Music, 1999.
Best-selling record by Sugar Ray in the album *14:59* (Lava/Atlantic, 98).

Everybody's Free (to Wear Sunscreen)
Words and music by Tim Cox and Nigel Swanston.
Peermusic Ltd., 1995.
Best-selling record by Baz Luhrman in the album *Something for Everybody* (Capitol, 99). Lyrics for song originated as a speech by Chicago journalist Mary Schmich. It was originally thought to be a graduation address by author Kurt Vonnegut and was widely reported as such over the Internet. The music for this song first appeared in the recent film Romeo & Juliet.

Everything Is Everything
Words and music by Lauryn Hill and Johari Newton.
Sony ATV Music, 1998/Obverse Creation Music, 1998/Jermaine Music, 1998.
Best-selling record by Lauryn Hill in the album *The MisEducation of Lauryn Hill* (Ruffhouse/Columbia, 98).

Ex-Factor
Words and music by Lauryn Hill, Alan Bergman, Marilyn Bergman, Marvin Hamlisch, Robert Diggs, Dennis Coles, Greg Grice, and Corey Woods.
Sony ATV Music, 1998/Obverse Creation Music, 1998/Colgems-EMI Music, 1998/Careers-BMG Music, 1999/Wu-Tang Music, 1999.
Best-selling record by Lauryn Hill in the album *The MisEducation of Lauryn Hill* (Ruffhouse/Columbia, 98).

Exhibit A
Words and music by Stephen Sondheim.
Burthen Music Co., Inc., 1954.
Revived by Charles Karvelas in the musical *Saturday Night*.

Eyes of a Child
Words and music by Trey Parker and Marc Shaiman.
Introduced by Michael McDonald in the film and soundtrack album *South Park: Bigger, Longer & Uncut* (Atlantic, 99).

F

Faded Pictures
Words and music by Joe Thomas and Joshua Thompson.
Zomba Music, 1999/Keily Music, 1999/Tallest Tree Music, 1999/WB
Music, 1999.
Best-selling record by Case Woodard & Joe in the album *Personal
Conversation* (Def Jam/Mercury, 98). Introduced in the movie Rush
Hour.

Faith of the Heart
Words and music by Diane Warren.
Realsongs, 1999.
Best-selling record by Rod Stewart in the film and soundtrack album
Patch Adams (Universal Soundtrack, 99).

Faith in You
Words and music by Matthew Sweet.
Charm Trap Music, 1999/EMI-Blackwood Music Inc., 1999.
Introduced by Matthew Sweet in the album *In Reverse* (Volcano, 99).

Falling Away from Me
Words and music by Korn.
Best-selling record by Korn in the album *Issues* (Immortal/Epic, 99).

Falls Apart
Words and music by Sugar Ray, David Kahne, Matthew Karges, Mark
McGrath, Charles Frazier, Joseph Nichol, and Rodney Sheppard.
E Equals Music, 1999/Grave Lack of Talent Music, 1999/WB Music,
1999.
Best-selling record by Sugar Ray in the album *14:59* (Lava/Atlantic,
98).

Fast as You Can
Words and music by Fiona Apple.
FHW Music, Beverly Hills, 1999.

Introduced by Fiona Apple in the album *When the Pawn..* (Columbia, 99).

Feels Like Home
Words and music by Randy Newman.
Randy Newman Music, 1995.
Revived by Emmylou Harris, Linda Ronstadt and Dolly Parton in the album *Trio II* (Asylum, 99).

15 Minutes
Words and music by Nicolia Turman, Marc Nelson, Sam Salter, and Tab.
Pink Jeans Music, 1999/Zomba Music, 1999/Hit Co. South, 1999/A Salt on the Charts Music, 1999/Tabulous Music, 1999/Universal Music, 1999/Songs of Universal, 1999/Miti Music, 1999.
Best-selling record by Marc Nelson in the album *Chocolate Mood* (Columbia, 99).

Finding Home
Words and music by Ricky Ian Gordon and Tina Landau.
Introduced by Jessica McLaskey in the musical *Dreams True*.

For a Dancer
Words and music by Jackson Browne.
WB Music, 1972.
Introduced by Linda Ronstadt and Emmylou Harris in the album *Western Wall: The Tucson Sessions* (Asylum, 99).

For a Little While
Words and music by Phil Vassar, Stephen Mandile, and Jerry Vandiver.
Magnature Music, 1998/Family Style Music, 1998/Glacier Park Music, 1999/Moraine, 1999/Malaco Music Co., 1999/EMI-April Music, 1999/ Phil Vassar, 1999.
Best-selling record by Tim McGraw in the album *A Place in the Sun* (Curb, 98).

For the Movies
Words and music by Buckcherry and Joshua Todd.
Lit Up Music, 1999/Famous Music Corp., 1999.
Introduced by Buckcherry in the album *Buckcherry* (DreamWorks, 99).

Forget About It
Words and music by R. L. Kass (pseudonym for Robert Castleman).
Sixteen Stars Music, 1999.
Introduced by Alison Krauss in the album *Forget About It* (Rounder, 99).

Fortunate
Words and music by Robert Kelly.

R. Kelly Music, 1999/Zomba Music, 1999.
Best-selling record by Maxwell in the film and soundtrack album *Life* (Loud/Interscope, 99).

4, 5, 6
Words and music by Christopher Stewart, Kandi Burruss, Tonya Johnston, and Jeffrey Jermaine Thompkins.
Famous Music Corp., 1999/Tunes on the Verge of Insanity, 1999/Mo Better Grooves Music, 1999/Kandacy Music, 1999/Jimi-Lane Music, 1999/Honey from Missouri Music, 1999/Money Mack Music, 1999/ EMI-April Music, 1999.
Best-selling record by Sole featuring J. T. Money & Kandi in the album *Skin Deep* (Dreamworks, 99).

Freak of the Week
Words and music by Butch Walker.
WB Music, 1999.
Best-selling record by Marvelous 3 in the album *Hey Album* (Hi-Fi/ Elektra, 99).

Free Girl Now
Words and music by Tom Petty.
Adria K Music, 1999/Wixen Music, 1999.
Best-selling record by Tom Petty in the album *Echo* (Warner Brothers, 99).

Freedom's Child
Words and music by Frank Wildhorn.
Introduced by Cast of the musical *The Civil War* (, 99).

Fur Slippers
Words and music by Bob Dylan (pseudonym for Robert Allen Zimmerman).
Special Rider Music, 1999.
Introduced by B. B. King in the TV show and soundtrack album *Shake, Rattle & Roll* (MCA, 99).

G

Genie in a Bottle
Words and music by Steve Kipner, David Frank, and Pam Sheyne.
Stephen A. Kipner Music, 1999/EMI-April Music, 1999/Appletree
   Music, 1999/Griff Griff Music, 1999/WB Music, 1999/Warner-
   Tamerlane Music, 1999.
Best-selling record by Christina Aguilera in the album *Christina
   Aguilera* (RCA, 99).

Get Born Again
Words and music by Jerry Cantrell and Layne Staley.
Lungclam Music, 1999/Buttnugget Publishing, 1999.
Best-selling record by Alice in Chains in the album *Nothing Safe: The
   Best of the Box* (Columbia, 99).

Get Gone
Words and music by Johnta Austin, Brian Cox, and Kevin Hicks.
Naked Under My Clothes Music, 1999/Chrysalis Music Group, 1999/
   Baby Little Music, 1999/Koh Music, 1999/Noontime Music, 1999.
Best-selling record by Ideal in the album *Ideal* (Noon Time/Virgin, 99).

Get It on Tonite (American-German)
English words and music by Montell Jordan, Sergio Moore, D. Benbow,
   A. Wilson, J. Evers, Brian Palmer, and Jurgen Korduletsch.
EMI Unart Music, 1999/Famous Music Corp., 1999/Chubby Music,
   1999/PLX Music, 1999/Tobaki Music, 1999/Levar's Cribb Music,
   1999/Warner-Chappell Music, 1999.
Best-selling record by Montell Jordan in the album *Get It on Tonite*
   (Def Soul, 99).

Get in Line (Canadian)
Words and music by Stephen Page and Elliott Robertson.
Variety Music Inc., 1999/TCF Music, 1999/Treat Baker Music, 1999.
Introduced by Barenaked Ladies in the TV show and soundtrack album
   King of the Hill (Reprise, 99).

Ghost in This House
Words and music by Hugh Prestwood.
Careers-BMG Music, 1990/Hugh Prestwood, 1990.
Revived by Alison Krauss in the album *Forget About It* (Rounder, 99).
  Introduced by Shenandoah.

A Girl Named Happiness (Never Been Kissed)
Words and music by Jeremy Jordan and Chuck Luongo.
Introduced by Jeremy Jordan in the film and soundtrack album *Never
  Been Kissed* (Capital, 99).

Girl on TV
Words and music by Rich Cronin, Brad Young, and Dow Brain.
Trans Continental Music, 1999/D&W Tone Music, 1999/BKY Music,
  1999.
Best-selling record by LFO in the album *LFO* (Arista, 99).

Girl's Best Friend
Words and music by Sean Carter, Kasseem Dean, and Mashonda
  Tifrere.
Karima Music, 1999/Warner-Tamerlane Music, 1999/Lil Lu Lu Music,
  1999/EMI-Blackwood Music Inc., 1999/Colpix, 1999/Sony ATV
  Songs, 1999/Swizz Beats Music, 1999/Dead Game Music, 1999.
Introduced by Jay Z in the film and soundtrack album *Blue Streak*
  (Epic, 99).

Give It to You
Words and music by James Harris, III, Terry Lewis, Jordan Knight, and
  Robin Thicke.
Flyte Tyme Tunes, 1999/EMI-April Music, 1999/Jordan Knight Music,
  1999/I Like Em Thicke Music, 1999.
Best-selling record by Jordan Knight in the album *Jordan Knight*
  (Interscope, 99).

God Must Have Spent a Little More Time on You
Words and music by Carl Sturken and Evan Rodgers.
Universal Music Corp., 1999/Bayjun Beat, 1999.
Best-selling record by 'N Sync in the album *'N Sync* (RCA, 98).
  Revived by Alabama and 'N Sync in the album *Twentieth Century*
  (RCA Nashville, 99).

Gone Crazy
Words and music by Alan Jackson.
Yee Haw Music, Nashville, 1998/WB Music, 1998.
Best-selling record by Alan Jackson in the album *High Mileage* (Arista
  Nashville, 98).

Got Your Money
Words and music by Pharrell Williams, Chad Hugo, and Russell Jones.

The Waters of Nazareth Music, 1999/EMI-Blackwood Music Inc., 1999/
    Chase Chad Music, 1999/EMI-April Music, 1999/Old Dirty Music,
    1999/Warner-Tamerlane Music, 1999.
Best-selling record by Ol' Dirty Bastard featuring Kelis in the album
    Nigga Please (Elektra, 99).

Gotta Man
Words and music by Eve Jeffers, Kasseem Dean, and Mashonda Tifrere.
Warner-Tamerlane Music, 1999/Dead Game Music, 1999/Swizz Beats
    Music, 1999/Blondie Rockwell Music, 1999/Karima Music, 1999.
Best-selling record by Eve in the album *Ruff Ryder's First Lady* (Ruff
    Ryders/Interscope, 99).

The Great Beyond
Words and music by Michael Stipe, Peter Buck, and Mike Mills.
Temporary Music, 1999.
Introduced by R.E.M. in the film and soundtrack album *Man on the
    Moon* (Warner Brothers/Jersey, 99).

Greatest Romance Ever Sold
Words and music by Prince (pseudonym for Prince Rogers Nelson).
Emancipated Music, 1999.
Best-selling record by Prince in the album *Rave un2 the Joy Fantastic*
    (Arista, 99).

Guerrilla Radio
Words and music by Timothy Commerford, Tom Morello, Brad Wilk,
    and Zack De La Rocha.
Sony ATV Songs, 1999/Retribution Music, 1999.
Best-selling record by Rage Against the Machine in the album *TheBattle
    of Los Angeles* (Epic, 99).

H

Hands of a Working Man
Words and music by David Williams and Jim Collins.
Sugar Bend Music, 1999/Meg Alex Music, 1999/Warner-Tamerlane
    Music, 1999.
Best-selling record by Ty Herndon in the album *Steam* (Epic, 99).

Hanging Around
Words and music by Adam Duritz, David Bryson, Dan Vickrey, and
    Ben Mize.
EMI-Blackwood Music Inc., 1999/Jones Fall Music, 1999.
Best-selling record by Counting Crows in the album *This Desert Life*
    DGC/Interscope, 99).

Happily Ever After
Words and music by Case Woodard and Christopher Henderson.
Baby Spike Music, 1999/Gifted Source Music, 1999.
Best-selling record by Case Woodard in the album *Personal
    Conversation* (Def Jam, 99).

Hard on Me (English)
Words and music by Richard Thompson.
Beeswing Music, 1999.
Introduced by Richard Thompson in the album *Mock Tudor* (Capitol,
    99).

The Hardest Thing
Words and music by Steve Kipner and David Frank.
Stephen A. Kipner Music, 1999/EMI-April Music, 1999.
Best-selling record by 98 Degrees in the album *98 and Rising*
    (Universal, 99).

He Can't Love You
Words and music by Brian Casey, Brandon Casey, and Cox.
Them Damn Twins Music, 1999/Babyboy's Little Music, 1999/
    Noontime Music, 1999.

Best-selling record by Jagged Edge in the album *J. E. Heartbreak* (So So Def/Columbia, 99).

He Didn't Have to Be
Words and music by Kelly Lovelace and Brad Paisley.
EMI-April Music, 1999/Sea Bayle Music, 1999/Love Ranch Music, 1999.
Best-selling record by Brad Paisley in the album *Who Needs Pictures* (Arista Nashville, 99).

Heartbreak Hotel
Words and music by Carsten Schack, Kenneth Karlin, and Tamara Savage.
Jungle Fever Music, 1999/EMI-Blackwood Music Inc., 1999/EMI Solvang Music, 1999/Marshall Music, 1999/EMI-April Music, 1999.
Best-selling record by Whitney Houston in the album *My Love Is Your Love* (Arista, 98).Nominated for a Grammy Award, Best R&B Song of the Year, 1999.

Heartbreaker
Words and music by Mariah Carey, Shirley Elliston, Lincoln Chase, Narada Michael Walden, and Jeffrey Cohen.
Sony ATV Songs, 1999/Rye Songs, 1999/EMI-Blackwood Music Inc., 1999/Lil Lu Lu Music, 1999/Al Gallico Music Corp., 1999/WB Music, 1999/When Worlds Collide, 1999/See No Evil Music, 1999.
Best-selling record by Mariah Carey featuring Jay Z in the album *Butterfly* (Columbia, 99).

Heavy
Words and music by Ed Roland.
Sparrow Song Music, 1999/Colgems-EMI Music, 1999.
Best-selling record by Collective Soul in the album *Dosage* (Atlantic, 99).

Hey Leonardo (She Likes Me for Me)
Words and music by Elliot Sloan, Jeff Pence, and Emosia.
Tosha Music, 1999/EMI-April Music, 1999/Shapiro, Bernstein & Co., Inc., 1999.
Best-selling record by Blessid Union of Souls in the album *Walking off the Buzz* (Push/V2, 99).

High Fashion Queen
Words and music by Gram Parsons and Chris Parsons.
Irving Music Inc., 1970.
Revived by Chris Hillman and Steve Earle in the album *Return of the Grievous Angel: A Tribute to Gram Parsons* (Almo Sounds, 99).

Higher
Words and music by Mark Tremonti and Scott Stapp.

Stapp/Tremonti Music, New York, 1999/Dwight Frye, 1999.
Best-selling record by Creed in the album *Human Clay* (Wind Up, 99).

Highway to Hell (English)
Words and music by Angus Young and Bon Scott.
J. Albert & Sons Music, 1979.
Revived by Marilyn Manson in the film and soundtrack album *Detroit Rock City* (Mercury, 99).

Hillbilly Shoes
Words and music by Mike Geiger, Woody Mullis, and Bobby Taylor.
Sixteen Stars Music, 1999.
Best-selling record by Montgomery Gentry in the album *Tattoos and Scars* (Columbia, 99).

Hold on Hope
Words and music by Robert Pollard.
Sang Melee Music, 1999.
Introduced by Guided by Voices in the album *Do the Collapse* (TVT, 99).

Hold Me
Words and music by Brian McKnight, Samuel Barnes, and Jean Claude Olivier.
Tricky Track Music, Piermont, 1999/Songs of Polygram, 1999/Cancelled Lunch Music, 1999/Slam U Well Music, 1999/Twelve & Under Music, 1999/Jelly's Jams L.L.C. Music, 1999/Jumping Bean Music, 1999.
Best-selling record by Brian McKnight featuring Tone and Kobe Bryant in the album *Back at One* (Motown, 99).

Hold on to Me
Words and music by Eric Blair Daly and William Rambeaux.
Reynsong Music, 1999/Bayou Bay Music, 1999.
Best-selling record by John Michael Montgomery in the album *Home to You* (Atlantic, 99).

Hold On
Words and music by Tom Waits.
Jalma Music, 1999.
Introduced by Tom Waits in the album *Mule Variations* (Epitaph, 99).

Holla Holla
Words and music by Jeffrey Atkins, T. Green, and Irving Lorenzo.
TVT, NYC, 1999/DJ Irv, 1999.
Best-selling record by Ja Rule in the album *Venni, Vetti, Vecci* (Murder Inc/Def Jam/Mercury, 99).

Home to You
Words and music by Sara Light and Arlen Smith.
Arlos Smith Music, 1999/Good Ol Delta Boys Music, 1999/Zamalama
Music, 1999.
Best-selling record by John Michael Montgomery in the album *Home to
You* (Atlantic, 99).

Hot Boyz
Words and music by Missy Elliott (pseudonym for Melissa Elliott) and
Tim Mosley.
Mass Confusion Music, 1999/WB Music, 1999/Virginia Beach Music,
1999.
Best-selling record by Missy "Misdemeanor" Elliott featuring Nas, Eve
and Q-Tip in the album *Da Real World* (The Gold Mind/East West,
99).

House Where Nobody Lives
Words and music by Tom Waits.
Jalma Music, 1999.
Introduced by Tom Waits in the album *Mule Variations* (Epitaph, 99).

How Do I Deal
Words and music by Dillon O'Brien, Phil Roy, and Bob Jr. Thiele.
Warner-Tamerlane Music, 1999/Paradise Ave. Music, 1999/The Phil
Roy Music, 1999/Owen Pop Music, 1999.
Introduced by Jennifer Love Hewitt in the film and soundtrack album *I
Still Know What You Did Last Summer* (Warner Brothers, 99).

How Forever Feels
Words and music by Wendell Mobley and Tony Mullins.
Warner-Tamerlane Music, 1999/New Works Music, 1999/WB Music,
1999.
Best-selling record by Kenny Chesney in the album *Everywhere We Go*
(BNA, 99).

I

I Ain't Marchin' Anymore
Words and music by Phil Ochs.
Barricade Music Inc., 1964.
Revived by Black 47 in the album *Bleecker Street: Greenwich Village in the '60s* (Astor Place, 99).

I Already Know
Words and music by Jason Falkner.
Introduced by Jason Falkner in the album *Can You Still Feel* (Elektra, 99).

I Already Loved You
Words and music by Jim Lauderdale.
Laudersongs, 1999.
Introduced by Jim Lauderdale in the album *Onward Through It All* (RCA, 99).

I Can't Get over You
Words and music by Ronnie Dunn and Jim McBride.
Sony ATV Tree Publishing, 1999/Itchy Putschy, 1999/Warner-Tamerlane Music, 1999/Constant Pressure Music, 1999.
Best-selling record by Brooks & Dunn in the album *Tight Rope* (Arista, 99).

I Could Not Ask for More
Words and music by Diane Warren.
Realsongs, 1999.
Best-selling record by Edwin McCain in the film and soundtrack album *Message in a Bottle* (Lava/Atlantic, 99).

I Do (Cherish You)
Words and music by Keith Stegall and Dan Hill.
Big P Music, Baton Rouge, 1999/Smash Vegas, 1999/If Dreams Had Wings, 1999.

Revived by 98 Degrees in the film and soundtrack album *Nottinghill* (Universal, 99).

I Don't Want to Miss a Thing
Words and music by Diane Warren.
Realsongs, 1998.
Revived by Mark Chesnutt in the album *I Don't Want to Miss a Thing* (Decca, 99).

I Knew I Loved You (Australian)
Words and music by Darron Hayes and Daniel Jones.
Rough Cut Music, 1999/WB Music, 1999.
Best-selling record by Savage Garden in the album *Affirmation* (Columbia, 99).

I Know
Words and music by Fiona Apple.
FHW Music, Beverly Hills, 1999.
Introduced by Fiona Apple in the album *When the Pawn..* (Columbia, 99).

I Learned from the Best
Words and music by Diane Warren.
Realsongs, 1999.
Best-selling record by Whitney Houston in the album *My Love Is Your Love* (Arista, 99).

I Love You
Words and music by Tammy Hyler, Adrienne Follese, and Keith Follese.
Sony ATV Cross Keys Publishing Co. Inc., 1999/Encore Entertainment, 1999/Scott & Soda Music, 1999/Bud Dog Music, 1999/Follazoo Music, 1999.
Best-selling record by Martina McBride in the album *Emotion* (RCA Nashville, 99).

I Love You Came Too Late
Words and music by Eric Foster White and Michael Henry.
Zomba Music, 1999/4MW Music, 1999/Riddim Kingdom Music, 1999.
Best-selling record by Joey McIntyre in the album *Stay the Same* (Maverick, 99).

I Miss You
Words and music by Randy Newman.
Randy Newman Music, 1999.
Introduced by Randy Newman in the album *Bad Love* (DreamWorks, 99).

I Need to Know (Puerto Rican)
English words and music by Mark Anthony and Corey Rooney.
Sony ATV Songs, 1999/Cori Tiffani Music, 1999.
Best-selling record by Marc Anthony in the album *Marc Anthony*
  (Columbia, 99).

I Remember That
Words and music by Stephen Sondheim.
Burthen Music Co., Inc., 1954.
Revived by Samantha Fitchen in the musical *Saturday Night*.

I Try
Words and music by David Wilder, Jinsoo Lim, Jeremy Ruzumna, and
  Natalie McIntyre.
EMI-April Music, 1999/Jinsoo Lim Music, 1999/Roastitoasti Music,
  1999/Children of the Forest Music, 1999/Mel Boopie Music, 1999.
Introduced by Macy Gray in the album *On How Life Is* (MCA, 99).

I Wanna Love You Forever
Words and music by Sam Watters and L. Biancaniello.
EMI-April Music, 1999/27th and May Music, 1999/SMY Music, 1999.
Best-selling record by Jessica Simpson in the album *Sweet Kisses*
  (Columbia, 99).

I Want It All
Words and music by Warren Griffin, D. Robinson, E. Jordan, R.
  Debarge, and Eldra Debarge.
Warren G, 1999/WB Music, 1999/Warner-Chappell Music, 1999/Jobete
  Music Co., 1999.
Best-selling record by Warren G. in the album *I Want It All* (G-Funk/
  Restless, 99).

I Want It That Way (German)
English words and music by Max Martin and Andreas Carlsson.
Zomba Music, 1999/Grantsville, 1999.
Best-selling record by the Backstreet Boys in the album *Millennium*
  (Jive, 99).Nominated for Grammy Awards, Best Record of the Year,
  1999 and Best Song of the Year, 1999.

I Will Get There
Words and music by Diane Warren.
Realsongs, 1998.
Best-selling record by Boyz II Men in the film and soundtrack album
  Prince of Egypt (Dreamworks/Geffen, 98).

I Will Remember You (Live)
Words and music by Sarah McLachlan, Seamus Ennis, and Dave
  Merenda.
Sony ATV Songs, 1995/Tyde, 1995/Seamus Ennis Music, 1995/Fox

Film Music Corp., 1995/Twentieth Century-Fox Music Corp., 1995.
Revived by Sarah McLachlan in the album *Mirror Ball* (Arista, 99).

If I Could Turn Back Time
Words and music by Robert Kelly.
Zomba Music, 1999/R. Kelly Music, 1999.
Best-selling record by R. Kelly in the album *R.* (Jive, 99).

If I Wrote You
Words and music by Dar Williams.
Burning Field Music, 1997.
Revived by Dar Williams in the album *Main Stage Live: Falcon Ridge
Folk Festival* (Signature Sounds, 99).

If You Had My Love
Words and music by Rodney Jerkins, Corey Rooney, LeShawn Daniels,
Fred Jerkins, and Jennifer Lopez.
EMI-Blackwood Music Inc., 1999/Ensign Music, 1999/Fred Jerkins
Publishing, 1999/Nuyorican Publishing, 1999/Rodney Jerkins Music,
1999/Sony ATV Songs, 1999.
Best-selling record by Jennifer Lopez in the album *On the 6* (Work, 99).

If You Leave Me
Words and music by Richard Marx.
Chi-Boy, 1999.
Best-selling record by Barbra Streisand and Vince Gill in the album *A
Love Like Ours* (Columbia, 99).

If You Love Me
Words and music by Keni Lewis.
EMI Hastings Music, 1999/EMI-April Music, 1999.
Best-selling record by Mint Condition in the album *Life's Aquarium*
(Elektra, 99).

If You (Lovin' Me)
Words and music by Kenny Dickerson, Antoinette Roberson, Lincoln
Browder, and Darrell Allamby.
2000 Watts Music, Newark, 1999/Divided, 1999/Toni Robi Music,
1999/Zomba Music, 1999/WB Music, 1999.
Best-selling record by Silk in the album *Tonight* (Elektra, 99).

I'll Go Crazy
Words and music by Andy Griggs, William Wilson, and Zack Turner.
Sony ATV Tree Publishing, 1999/Sony ATV Cross Keys Publishing Co.
Inc., 1999.
Best-selling record by Andy Griggs in the album *You Won't Ever Be
Lonely* (RCA Nashville, 99).

I'll Still Love You More
Words and music by Diane Warren.
Realsongs, 1998.
Best-selling record by Trisha Yearwood in the album *Where Your Road Leads* (MCA Nashville, 98).

I'll Think of a Reason Later
Words and music by Tony Martin and Tim Nichols.
Hamstein Cumberland, Nashville, 1999/Baby Mae Music, Austin, 1999/ EMI-Blackwood Music Inc., 1999/Tyland Music, 1999.
Best-selling record by Lee Ann Womack in the album *Some Things I Know* (Decca, 99).

I'm Already Taken
Words and music by Terry Ryan and Steve Wariner.
Fleetside Music, 1999/CMI America, 1999/Steve Wariner, 1999.
Best-selling record by Steve Wariner in the album *Two Teardrops* (Capitol, 99).

I'm Dead (But I Don't Know It)
Words and music by Randy Newman.
Randy Newman Music, 1999.
Introduced by Randy Newman in the album *Bad Love* (DreamWorks, 99).

I'm Gonna Be Strong
Words and music by Gene Pitney.
Screen Gems-EMI Music Inc., 1964.
Revived by Buddy Miller in the album *Cruel Moon* (Rounder, 99).

I'm Not Ready
Words and music by Keith Sweat, Joe Little, and Willie Jones.
Twisted Music, 1998/EMI-April Music, 1998/Lil Mob Music, 1998/ Divided, 1998/Zomba Music, 1998.
Best-selling record by Keith Sweat in the album *Still in the Game* (Elektra, 99).

I'm Past My Prime
Words and music by Johnny Mercer and Gene DePaul.
Commander Music, 1956/Hub Music, 1956.
Revived by Emily Skinner and Alice Ripley in the album *Unsuspecting Hearts* (Varese Sarabande, 99). Introduced in the musical Lil Abner.

I'm Still in Love with You
Words and music by Steve Earle.
WB Music, 1999.
Introduced by Steve Earle and Iris DeMent in the album *The Mountain* (K-Squared, 99).

In Spite of Ourselves
Words and music by John Prine.
Weowna Music, 1999.
Introduced by John Prine and Iris Dement in the film and soundtrack
  album *Daddy & Them* (Oh Boy, 99).

In 2 Deep
Words and music by Mark Selby, Kenny Wayne Shepherd, and Danny
  Tate.
Bro N' Sis Music, 1999/Come on In Music, 1999/Estes Park Music,
  1999/Only Hit Music, 1999.
Best-selling record by Kenny Wayne Shepherd Band in the album *Live
  On* (Giant/Reprise, 99).

Is This All
Words and music by Jonatha Brooke.
Dog Dream, 199 .
Revived by Jonatha Brooke in the album *Jonatha Brooke Live* (Bad
  Dog, 99).

It Ain't My Fault
Words and music by Silkk the Shocker (pseudonym for Zyshonne
  Miller) and Mystikal (pseudonym for Michael Tyler).
Big P Music, Baton Rouge, 1999.
Best-selling record by Silkk the Shocker featuring Mystikal in the album
  Made Man (No Limit/Priority, 99).

It's All About You (Not About Me)
Words and music by Carsten Schack, Kenneth Karlin, and Heavynn
  Lumpkins.
Jungle Fever Music, 1999/EMI Solvang Music, 1999/Designa Music,
  1999/Almo Music Corp., 1999/Light Gyrl Music, 1999.
Best-selling record by Tracie Spencer in the album *Tracie* (Capitol, 99).

It's Not Right But It's Okay
Words and music by Fred Jerkins, Rodney Jerkins, LeShawn Daniels,
  Isaac Phillips, and Tony Estes.
EMI-Blackwood Music Inc., 1999/Famous Music Corp., 1999/EMI-April
  Music, 1999/PLX Music, 1999/Zomba Music, 1999/MCA Music,
  1999/Little B, 1999/Leshawn Daniels, 1999.
Best-selling record by Whitney Houston in the album *My Love Is Your
  Love* (Arista, 99).Nominated for a Grammy Award, Best R&B Song
  of the Year, 1999.

It's Not over Yet
Words and music by Jason Robert Brown.
Revived by Brent Carver and Carolee Carmello in the original cast
  album *Parade* (RCA, 99).

I've Committed Murder

Words and music by Kilu Beckwith, Macy Gray, Jeremy Ruzumna, and Gregg Swann.

EMI-April Music, 1999.

Introduced by Macy Gray in the album *On How Life Is* (Epic, 99).

J

Jamboree
Words and music by Keir Gist, Vinnie Brown, Anthony Chriss, and
  Benny Golson.
Celedia Music, 1999/Warner-Tamerlane Music, 1999.
Best-selling record by Naughty By Nature featuring Zhane in the album
  19 Naughty Nine: Nature's Fury (Arista, 99).

Jigga My N..
Words and music by Sean Carter and Kasseem Dean.
EMI-Blackwood Music Inc., 1999/Lil Lu Lu Music, 1999.
Best-selling record by Jay Z in the album *Ryde or Die Compilation*
  (Rock-A-Fella/Ruff Ryders/Interscope, 99).

Joe van Gogh
Words and music by Dan Bern.
Kababa Music, Los Angeles, 1999.
Introduced by Dan Bern in the album *Smartie Mine* (DBNQ, 99).

Jukebox
Words and music by Ani DiFranco.
Righteous Babe Music, Buffalo, 1999.
Introduced by Ani DiFranco in the album *Up Up Up Up Up Up*
  (Righteous Babe, 99).

Just Wave Hello (Irish)
Words and music by Danny Beckerman.
Introduced by Charlotte Church in the album *Charlotte Church*(Sony
  Classical, 99). Used as the millennium anthem for the Ford Motor
  Company.

K

Keep Away
Words and music by Sully Erna.
MCA Music, 1999.
Best-selling record by Godsmack in the album *Godsmack* (Warner
  Brothers, 99).

King of Pain
Words and music by Sting (pseudonym for Gordon Sumner).
EMI-Blackwood Music Inc., 1983/Magnetic Music Publishing Co.,
  1982.
Revived by Alanis Morissette in the album *MTV Unplugged* (Maverick,
  99).

Kiss Me
Words and music by Matt Slocum.
Partnt Music, 1998/My So Called Music, 1998.
Best-selling record by Sixpence None the Richer in the film and
  soundtrack album *She's All That* (Squint/Columbia, 98).

Krautmeyer
Words and music by Dan Bern.
Kababa Music, Los Angeles, 1999.
Introduced by Dan Bern in the album *Smartie Mine* (DBHQ, 99).

L

L.A. Song
Words and music by Beth Hart.
Jezebel Blues Music, 1999.
Introduced by Beth Hart in the album *Screaming for My Supper* (143/
  Lava/Atlantic, 99).

Larger Than Life (German)
English words and music by Max Martin, Kristian Lundin, and Brian
  Littrell.
Zomba Music, 1999/Grantsville, 1999/B-Rok Music, 1999.
Best-selling record by the Backstreet Boys in the album *Millennium*
  (Jive, 99).

The Last Balloon (English)
Words and music by Andy Partridge.
Virgin Music, 1999.
Introduced by XTC in the album *Apple Venus Volume 1* (Idea/TVT, 99).

Last Kiss
Words and music by Wayne Cochran.
Trio Music Co., Inc., 1964/Fort Knox Music Co., 1964.
Revived by Pearl Jam in the album *NoBoundaries* (Epic, 99).

Laughing at Life
Words and music by Nick Kenny, Charles Kenny, and Cornell Todd.
M. Witmark & Sons, 1930.
Revived by Susannah McCorkle in the album *From Broken Hearts to
  Blue Skies* (Concord Jazz, 99).

Lay Down (Candles in the Rain)
Words and music by Melanie Safka.
Bienstock Publishing Co., 1970/Jerry Leiber Music, 1970/Mike Stoller
  Music, 1970.
Revived by Meredith Brooks and Queen Latifah in the album
  Deconstruction (Capitol, 99).

Learn to Fly
Words and music by Foo Fighters.
MJ12 Music, 1999/Flying Earform, 1999/Living Under a Rock Music,
  1999/Virgin Music, 1999.
Best-selling record by Foo Fighters in the album *There Is Nothing Left
  to Lose* (Roswell/RCA, 99).

Lesson in Leavin'
Words and music by Randy Goodrum and Brent Maher.
Chappell & Co., Inc., 1970/Sailmaker Music, 1970/Sony ATV Cross
  Keys Publishing Co. Inc., 1970/Blue Quill Music, 1970.
Revived by Jo Dee Messina in the album *I'm Alright* (Curb, 98).

Lit Up
Words and music by Buckcherry and Joshua Todd.
Lit Up Music, 1999/Famous Music Corp., 1999.
Best-selling record by Buckcherry in the album *Buckcherry*
  (Dreamworks, 99).

Little Goodbyes
Words and music by Jason Deere, Kenny Greenberg, and Kristyn
  Osborn.
Colonel Rebel Music, 1999/Kentucky Thunder Music, 1999/Rushing
  Water Music, 1999/Without Anna Music, 1999/Magnolia Hill Music,
  1999/Kent Greene Music, 1999/Sony ATV Tree Publishing, 1999.
Best-selling record by Shedaisy in the album *The Whole Shebang* (Lyric
  Street, 99).

Little Man
Words and music by Alan Jackson.
Yee Haw Music, Nashville, 1999/WB Music, 1999.
Best-selling record by Alan Jackson in the album *High Mileage* (Arista
  Nashville, 99).

Livin' La Vida Loca (American-Puerto Rican)
English words and music by Robi Rosa and Desmond Child.
A Phantom Vox Music, 1999/Warner-Tamerlane Music, 1999/
  Desmophobia, 1999/Shobi Music, 1999.
Best-selling record by Ricky Martin in the album *Ricky Martin* (Sony,
  99).Nominated for Grammy Awards, Best Record of the Year, 1999
  and Best Song of the Year, 1999.

Lonely and Gone
Words and music by Greg Crowe, Dave Gibson, and Bill McCorvey.
House of Integrity Music, 1999/Little Tomatoes Music, 1999/Nomad-
  Noman Music, 1999/Songs of Polygram, 1999.
Best-selling record by Montgomery Gentry in the album *Tattoos and
  Scars* (Columbia, 99).

Lonesome Town
Words and music by Baker Knight.
EMI Unart Music, 1958/Matragun Music Inc., 1958.
Revived by by Paul McCartney in the album *Run Devil Run* (Capitol, 99).

Looking for Answers
Words and music by Susan Tedeschi.
Cooltonic Music, 1999.
Introduced by Susan Tedeschi in the album *Just Won't Burn* (Tone-Cool, 99).

Looking Forward
Words and music by Neil Young.
Silver Fiddle, 1999.
Introduced by Crosby, Stills, Nash & Young in the album *Looking Forward* (Reprise, 99).

Losing Hand
Words and music by Charles Calhoun.
Unichappell Music Inc., 1954.
Revived by Susannah McCorkle in the album *From Broken Hearts to Blue Skies* (Concord Jazz, 99). Introduced by Ray Charles.

Lost in You
Words and music by Gordon Kennedy, Wayne Kirkpatrick, and Tommy Sims.
Shobi Music, 1999/Sundance Kid Music, 1999/BMG Music, 1999/Warner-Tamerlane Music, 1999/Sell the Cow Music, 1999.
Best-selling record by Garth Brooks as Chris Gaines in the album *In the Life of Chris Gaines* (Capitol, 99).

Love Abides
Words and music by Tom Russell.
Frontera Music, 1999.
Best-selling record by Tom Russell in the album *The Man from God Knows Where* (Hightone, 99).

Love All over Again
Words and music by Volt Renn and Jolyon Skinner.
Zomba Music, 1999/Conversation Tree Music, 1999.
Best-selling record by Michael Fredo in the album *Introducing Michael Fredo* (Ah/Warner Brothers/Qwest, 99).

Love Is All That Matters
Words and music by Diane Warren.
Realsongs, 1999.
Introduced by Diana Ross in the film *Double Platinum* and featured on her album *Every Day Is a New Day* (Motown, 99).

Love Keep Us Together
Words and music by Martin Sexton and Wayne Cohen.
Sony ATV Music, 1999/Wayne's World Music, 1999.
Introduced by Martin Sexton in the album *The American* (Atlantic, 99).

Love of My Life
Words and music by Carlos Santana and Dave Matthews.
Colden Grey Music, New York, 1999/Stellabella Music, 1999.
Introduced by Santana and Dave Matthews in the album *Supernatural*
(Arista, 99).

Love Song (Canadian)
Words and music by James Renald and Antoine Sicotte.
Sky Music, 1999/EMI-Blackwood Music Inc., 1999.
Best-selling record by Sky in the album *Piece of Paradise* (Arista, 99).

Loving You Is All I Know
Words and music by Diane Warren.
Realsongs, 1999.
Best-selling record by Pretenders in the film and soundtrack album *The
Other Sister* (Hollywood, 99).

M

The Magdelene Laundries
Words and music by Joni Mitchell.
Crazy Crow Music, 1998/Sony ATV Songs, 1998.
Introduced by Joni Mitchell and the Chieftains in the album *Tears of Stone* (RCA, 99).

Major Leagues
Words and music by Stephen Malkmus.
Treble Kicker Music, 1999.
Introduced by Pavement in the album *Terror Twilight* (Matador, 99).

Making Time
Words and music by Eddie Phillips and Ken Pickett.
EMI Unart Music, 1966/Orbit Music, 1966.
Revived by Creation in the film and soundtrack album *Rushmore* (London, 99).

Mambo No. 5 (A Little Bit of..) (German)
English words and music by Perez Prado, Lou Bega, and Zippy.
Peermusic Ltd., 1999.
Best-selling record by Lou Bega in the album *A Little Bit of Mambo* (RCA, 99).

Man I Feel Like a Woman
Words and music by Shania Twain and Robert John Lange.
Songs of Polygram, 1999/Loon Echo Music, 1999/Zomba Music, 1999.
Best-selling record by Shania Twain in the album *Come on Over* (Mercury Nashville, 98).

Maria
Words and music by Jimmy Destri.
Dick Johnson Music, 1999.
Best-selling record by Blondie in the album *No Exit* (Logic/Beyond, 98).

Marilyn and Joe
Words and music by Kinky Friedman (pseudonym for Richard F.

Friedman) and Sharon Rucker.
MCA Music, 1979/EMI Music Publishing.
Revived by Kinky Friedman and Kacey Jones in the album *Pearls in the Snow: The Songs of Kinky Friedman* (Beyond, 99).

Mas Tequila
Words and music by Sammy Hagar, Michael Farr, Paul Gadd, Gary Glitter, and Mike Leander.
WB Music, 1999/Songs of Universal, 1999.
Best-selling record by Sammy Hagar in the album *Red Voodoo* (MCA, 99).

Meanwhile
Words and music by Fred Knobloch and Wayland Holyfield.
J. Fred Knoblock Music, 1999/Waysong Music, 1999/Lebrun Ingram Music, 1999.
Best-selling record by George Strait in the album *Always Never the Same* (MCA Nashville, 98).

Meet Virginia
Words and music by Charlie Colin, Rob Hotchkiss, Patrick Monahan, Jimmy Stafford, and Scott Underwood.
Lo Giene Music, 1999/Leaning Tower Music, 1999/Wunderworld Music, 1999/Timon Music, 1999/Jaywood Music, 1999/EMI-Blackwood Music Inc., 1999.
Best-selling record by Train in the album *Train* (Aware/Columbia, 99).

Millennium
Words and music by Robbie Williams, Guy Chambers, Leslie Bricusse, and John Barry.
EMI Unart Music, 1999.
Best-selling record by Robbie Williams in the album *The Ego Has Landed* (Capitol, 99).

Moment of Weakness (Canadian)
Words and music by Beth Hopkins and Peter Karroll.
Kar Tay Music, 1999/Tay Kar Music, 1999.
Best-selling record by Bif Naked in the album *I Bificus* (Lava/Atlantic, 99).

Momentum
Words and music by Aimee Mann.
Aimee Mann, 1999.
Introduced by Aimee Mann in the film and soundtrack album *Magnolia* (Reprise, 99).

Movie Magg
Words and music by Carl Perkins.

Carl Perkins Music, 1957/Unichappell Music Inc., 1957.
Revived by Paul McCartney in the album *Run Devil Run* (Capitol, 99).

Mudshovel
Words and music by Johnny April, Aaron Lewis, Mike Mushok, and Jim Wysocki.
Best-selling record by Staind in the album *Dysfunction* (Flip/Elektra, 99).

Music of My Heart
Words and music by Diane Warren.
Realsongs, 1999.
Best-selling record by Gloria Estefan and 'N Sync in the film and soundtrack album *Music of the Heart* (Epic, 99).Nominated for an Academy Award, Best Song of the Year, 1999;Nominated for an Academy Award, Best Song of the Year, 1999; a Grammy Award, Best Song Written for a Movie, 1999.

Music That Makes Me Dance
Words and music by Jule Styne and Bob Merrill.
Chappell & Co., Inc., 1964.
Revived by Barbra Streisand in the album *A Love Like Ours* (Columbia, 99).

My Country
Words and music by Randy Newman.
Randy Newman Music, 1999.
Introduced by Randy Newman in the album *Bad Love* (Dreamworks, 99).

My Favorite Girl
Words and music by Steven A. Jordan, Dave Hollister, Sonnyboy Turpin (pseudonym for William Turpin), and Marc Kinchen.
Steven A. Jordan Music, 1999/WB Music, 1999/Oh God Music, 1999/ Polygram Music Publishing Inc., 1999/C. Israel Music, 1999/Big on Blue Music, 1999/Warner-Tamerlane Music, 1999.
Best-selling record by Dave Hollister in the album *Ghetto Hymns* (Def Squad/Dreamworks, 99).

My First Night with You
Words and music by Babyface (pseudonym for Kenny Edmunds) and Diane Warren.
Ecaf Music, 1999/Realsongs, 1999/Sony ATV Songs, 1999.
Best-selling record by Mya in the album *Mya* (University/Interscope, 99).

My Love Is Your Love
Words and music by Wyclef Jean and Jerry Duplesis.
Sony ATV Songs, 1999/Huss-Zwingli Music, 1999/Te Bass, 1999/EMI-

Blackwood Music Inc., 1999.
Best-selling record by Whitney Houston in the album *My Love Is Your Love* (Arista, 99).

My Name Is
Words and music by Claudius Siffre.
Chrysalis Music Group, 1999.
Best-selling record by Eminem in the album *The Slim Shady Lp* (Web/Aftermath/Interscope, 99).

My New Philosophy
Words and music by Andrew Lippa.
Revived by Sally Brown and Kristen Chenoweth in the musical *You're a Good Man Charley Brown*

My Own Worst Enemy
Words and music by Jeremy Popoff, Alan Popoff, Allen Shellenberger, and Kevin Baldes.
EMI-April Music, 1999/Jagermeister Music, 1999.
Best-selling record by Lit in the album *A Place in the Sun* (RCA, 99).

My Ritual
Words and music by Lou Barlow, John Davis, and Wally Gagel.
Bliss WG Music, 1999/Careers-BMG Music, 1999/Endless Soft Hits Music, 1999.
Introduced by the Folk Implosion in the album *One Part Lullaby* (Interscope, 99).

N

Nervous Breakthrough
Words and music by Jill Cuniff, Kathy Schellenbach, and Viv Trimble.
EMI-April Music, 1999.
Introduced by Luscious Jackson in the album *Electric Honey* (Grand
Royal/Capitol, 99).

Never Been Kissed
Words and music by Sherrie Austin, Will Rambeaux, and Greg Barnhill.
Reynsong Music, 1999/Lucky Ladybug Music, 1999/Chrysalis Music
Group, 1999/Audacity Music, 1999.
Best-selling record by Sherrie Austin in the album *Love in the Real
World* (Arista Nashville, 99).

Never Gonna Let You Go
Words and music by Babyface (pseudonym for Kenneth Edmunds) and
Damon Thomas.
Demis Music, 1999/EMI-April Music, 1999/EZ Music, 1999/Sony ATV
Songs, 1999/Ecaf Music, 1999.
Best-selling record by Faith Evans in the album *Keep the Faith* (Bad
Boy/Arista, 99).

New Girl
Words and music by Stephan Jenkins and Kevin Cadogan.
Cappagh Hill Music, 1999/Careers-BMG Music, 1999/EMI-Blackwood
Music Inc., 1999/3EB Music, 1999.
Introduced by Third Eye Blind in the film and soundtrack album
American Pie (Universal, 99).

New Ways to Dream (English)
Words and music by Andrew Lloyd Webber, Don Black, and James
Hampton Christopher.
Shobi Music, 1990.
Revived by Betty Buckley in the album *Betty Buckley's Broadway*
(Sterling, 99). From the musical Sunset Boulevard.

A Night to Remember
Words and music by Max T. Barnes and T. W. Hale.
Mike Curb Productions, 1999/Kinetic Diamond Music, 1999/Song of
    Peer, 1999/Gramily Music, 1999/Rob 'N Riley Music, 1999.
Best-selling record by Joe Diffie in the album *A Night to Remember*
    (Epic, 99).

No Leaf Clover
Words and music by James Hetfield, Kirk Hammett, and Lars Ulrich.
Creeping Death Music, 1999.
Best-selling record by Metallica in the album *S&M* (Elektra, 99).

No Matter What (English)
Words and music by Andrew Lloyd Webber and Jim Steinman.
Revived by Boyzone in the film and soundtrack album *Nottinghill*
    (Island, 99). Originated in the musical Whistle down the Wind.

No More Rain in This Cloud
Words and music by Gordon Chambers, Angie Stone, Jim Weatherly,
    and Bobby Williams.
Songs of Polygram, 1999/Polygram Music Publishing Inc., 1999/Hit Co.
    South, 1999/EMI-Full Keel Music, 1999/Lady Diamond Music, 1999/
    October 12th Music, 1999.
Best-selling record by Angie Stone in the album *Black Diamond* (Arista,
    99).

No Pigeons
Words and music by Howell, Ford, Bryan, Kevin Briggs, Kandi Burruss,
    and Tameka Kottle.
Sporty Music, 1999/Steel Burg Music, 1999/Commando Brabdo Music,
    1999/Safe Cracker Music, 1999/Shek' Em Down Music, 1999/Tam
    Music, 1999/Hitco Music, 1999/Jimi-Lane Music, 1999.
Best-selling record by Sporty Thievz featuring Mr. Woods in the album
    Street Cinema (Ruffhouse/Columbia, 99).

No Place That Far
Words and music by Sara Evans, Tom Shapiro, and Anthony Martin.
Hamstein Cumberland, Nashville, 1998/Baby Mae Music, Austin, 1998/
    Sony ATV Tree Publishing, 1998/Wenonga Music, 1998.
Best-selling record by Sara Evans in the album *No Place That Far*
    (RCA Nashville, 98).

No Pressure Over Cappucino
Words and music by Alanis Morissette and Nick Lashley.
Norick Music, Leona, 1999/Upward Dog Music, 1900.
Introduced by Alanis Morissette in the album *MTV Unplugged*
    (Maverick, 99).

No Scrubs
Words and music by Kevin Briggs, Kandi Burruss, and Tameka Kottle.
Shek' Em Down Music, 1999/Tam Music, 1999/Hitco Music, 1999/
Jimi-Lane Music, 1999/EMI-April Music, 1999/Kandacy Music, 1999/
Tony Mercedes Music, 1999/Windswept Pacific, 1999.
Best-selling record by TLC in the album *Fan Mail* (LaFace/Arista, 99)
.Won a Grammy Award for Best R&B Song of the Year 1999.
Nominated for a Grammy Award, Best Record of the Year, 1999.

Nookie
Words and music by William Durst, Wesley Borland, Samuel Rivers,
and John Otto.
Big Bizkit Music, 1999.
Best-selling record by Limp Bizkit in the album *Significant Other* (Flip/
Interscope, 99).

Not Me (English)
Words and music by Elton John and Tim Rice.
Happenstance Music, 1999/Sixty Four Square Music, 1999/Wonderland
Music, 1999.
Introduced by Boyz II Men in the album *Elton John's Aida* (Rocket,
99).

Nothing Can Keep Me from You
Words and music by Diane Warren.
Realsongs, 1999.
Introduced by Kiss in the film and soundtrack album *Detroit Rock City*
(Polygram, 99).

Nowadays
Words and music by John Kander and Fred Ebb.
Fiddleback, 1975/Kander & Ebb Inc., 1975.
Revived by Bebe Neuwirth and Karen Ziemba in the album *My Favorite
Broadway: The Leading Ladies Live at Carnegie Hall* (TVT/Hybrid,
99).

Number One
Words and music by Tommy Shaw.
Tranquility Base Songs, 1999.
Introduced by Styx in the album *Brave New World* (CMC, 99).

O

Oh My God
Words and music by Axl Rose.
Guns N' Roses Music, 1999.
Introduced by Guns N' Roses in the film and soundtrack album *End of Days* (Geffen, 99).

On the Bound
Words and music by Fiona Apple.
FHW Music, Beverly Hills, 1999.
Introduced by Fiona Apple in the album *When the Pawn..* (Columbia, 99).

One
Words and music by Harry Nilsson.
Unichappell Music Inc., 1968.
Revived by Aimee Mann in the film and soundtrack album *Magnolia* (Reprise, 99).

One
Words and music by Mark Tremonti and Scott Stapp.
Stapp/Tremonti Music, New York, 1999/Dwight Frye, 1999.
Best-selling record by Creed in the album *Human Clay* (Wind Up, 99).

One Bad Stud
Words and music by Jerry Leiber and Mike Stoller.
Jerry Leiber Music, 1955/Mike Stoller Music, 1955.
Revived by Brad Hawkins in the TV show and soundtrack album *Shake, Rattle & Roll* (MCA, 99). Originally popularized by the Blasters.

One Hundred Years from Now
Words and music by Gram Parsons.
Tickson Music, 1968/Wajoma Music, 1968.
Revived by Wilco in the album *Return of the Grievous Angel: A Tribute to Gram Parsons* (Almo Sounds, 99).

One More Try (English)
Words and music by George Michael and Geoff Overbig.
Morrison Leahy, England, 1987/Chappell & Co., Inc., 1987.
Revived by Divine in the album *Fairy Tales* (Pendulum/Red Ant, 98).

1999
Words and music by Prince (pseudonym for Prince Rogers Nelson).
Controversy Music, 1979/WB Music, 1979.
Revived by Prince as a single (Warner Brothers, 99).

1000 Oceans
Words and music by Tori Amos.
Sword and Stone Music, 1999.
Introduced by Tori Amos in the album *To Venus and Back* (Atlantic, 99).

Ooh La La (English)
Words and music by Ronnie Lane and Ron Wood.
WB Music, 1978.
Revived by the Faces in the film and soundtrack album *Rushmore* (London, 99).

Ooh Las Vegas
Words and music by Gram Parsons and Ric Grech.
Carbert Music Inc., 1974/Unichappell Music Inc., 1974/Wait and See Music, 1974.
Revived by Cowboy Junkies in the album *Return of the Grievous Angel: A Tribute to Gram Parsons* (Almo Sounds, 99).

Ordinary Heart
Words and music by Emmylou Harris and Kimmie Rhodes.
Gracey Rhodes Prod., 1999/Irving Music Inc., 1999.
Introduced by Emmylou Harris in the film and soundtrack album *Happy Texas* (Arista Austin, 99).

Ordinary Life
Words and music by Bonnie Baker and Connie Harrington.
McSpadden-Smith Music, 1999/Magnolia Hill Music, 1999.
Best-selling record by Chad Brock in the album *Chad Brock* (Warner Brothers Nashville, 99).

Out of Control
Words and music by Neil Young.
Silver Fiddle, 1999.
Introduced by CSNY in the album *Looking Forward* (Reprise, 99).

Out of My Head
Words and music by Tony Scalzo.
EMI-April Music, 1999.

Best-selling record by Fastball in the album *All the Pain Money Can Buy* (Hollywood, 99).

Out in the Streets
Words and music by Barry Mann and Cynthia Weil.
Screen Gems-EMI Music Inc., 1966/Tender Tunes Music Co., Inc., 1966/Trio Music Co., Inc., 1966/Songs of Polygram, 1966.
Revived by Blondie in the album *No Exit* (Beyond, 99).

P

Pacing the Cage (Canadian)
Words and music by Bruce Cockburn.
Golden Mountain Music Inc., 1997.
Revived by Jimmy Buffett in the album *Beach House on the Moon*
(Margaritaville/Island, 99).

Pack up Your Sorrows
Words and music by Richard Farina and Pauline Marsden.
Silkie Music, 1964/Songs of Polygram, 1964.
Revived by Loudon Wainwright and Iris Dement in the album *Bleecker*
Street: Greenwich Village in the '60s (Astor Place, 99).

Pain
Words and music by Terry Adams.
Music Sales Corp., 1999.
Introduced by NRBQ in the album *NRBQ* (Rounder, 99).

Paper Bag
Words and music by Fiona Apple.
FHW Music, Beverly Hills, 1999.
Introduced by Fiona Apple in the album *When the Pawn..* (Clean Slate/
Epic, 99).

Party Doll (English)
Words and music by Mick Jagger.
Promopub B. V., CH-1017 Amsterdam, Netherlands, 1987.
Revived by Mary Chapin Carpenter in the album *Party Doll and Other*
Favorites (Columbia, 99).

Pass in Time (Canadian)
Words and music by Beth Orton.
EMI-Blackwood Music Inc., 1999.
Introduced by Beth Orton and Terry Callier in the album *Central*
Reservation (DeConstruction/Arista, 99).

Please Remember Me
Words and music by Rodney Crowell and Will Jennings.
Sony ATV Cross Keys Publishing Co. Inc., 1999/Blue Sky Rider Songs, 1999/Irving Music Inc., 1999.
Best-selling record by Tim McGraw in the album *A Place in the Sun* (Curb, 99).

Pop a Top
Words and music by Nat Stuckey.
Sony ATV Tree Publishing, 1967.
Revived by Alan Jackson in the album *Under the Influence* (Arista Nashville, 99).

Popsicle Toes
Words and music by Michael Franks.
Warner-Tamerlane Music, 1976/Mississippi Mud Music, 1976.
Revived by Diana Krall in the album *When I Look in Your Eyes* (Verve, 99).

Porcelain
Words and music by Moby (pseudonym for Richard Melville Hall).
Warner-Tamerlane Music, 1999/Little Idiot Music, 1999.
Introduced by Moby in the album *Play* (V2, 99).

Powerful Thing
Words and music by Al Anderson and Sharon Vaughn.
Al Andersongs, Nashville, 1998/Mighty Nice Music, 1998/MCA Music, 1998/Fire Feather Music, 1998.
Best-selling record by Jo Dee Messina in the album *I'm Alright* (MCA Nashville, 98).

Praise You (English)
Words and music by Quentin Leo Cook and Camille Yarborough.
Polygram Music Publishing Inc., 1999/Matt Music, 1999/Songs of Universal, 1999.
Best-selling record by Fatboy Slim in the album *You've Come a Long Way Baby* (Skint/Astralwerks, 99).

The Promise
Words and music by Bruce Springsteen.
Bruce Springsteen Publishing, 1998.
Best-selling record by Bruce Springsteen in the album *18 Tracks* (Columbia, 99).Nominated for a Grammy Award, Best Rock Song of the Year, 1999.

Promises (English)
Words and music by Phil Collen and Robert John Lange.
Zomba Music, 1999.

Best-selling record by Def Leppard in the album *Euphoria* (Mercury, 99).

Put Your Lights On
Words and music by Everlast Schrody (pseudonym for Erik Schrody).
Slack A. D. Music, 1999/T-Boy Music Publishing Co., Inc., 1999.
Best-selling record by Santana featuring Everlast in the album
Supernatural (Arista, 99).

R

Race for the Prize
Words and music by Wayne Coyne, Steven Drozd, and Michael Ivins.
Lovely Sorts of Death Music, 1999/EMI-Blackwood Music Inc., 1999.
Introduced by the Flaming Lips in the album *The Soft Bulletin* (Warner
  Brothers, 99).

Rain Falls down in Amsterdam (Norwegian)
English words and music by Eric Andersen.
Deep Fork Music, Inc., 1999.
Introduced by Eric Anderson in the album *Memory of the Future*
  (Appleseed, 99).

Re-Arranged
Words and music by William Durst, Samuel Rivers, Wesley Borland,
  John Otto, Eric Barrier, Charles Bobbit, James Brown, Bobby Byrd,
  Leo Dimant, and William Griffin.
Big Bizkit Music, 1999/Crited Music, 1999/Robert Hill Music, 1999/
  Unichappell Music Inc., 1999/Songs of Polygram, 1999/Zomba
  Music, 1999.
Best-selling record by Limp Bizkit in the album *Significant Other* (Flip/
  Interscope, 99).

Ready or Not
Words and music by Martie Seidel and Marcus Hummon.
Careers-BMG Music, 1999/Floyd's Dream Music, 1999/Woolly Puddin'
  Music, 1999.
Best-selling record by the Dixie Chicks in the album *Fly* (Monument,
  99).

Ready to Run
Words and music by Marcus Hummon and Martie Seidel.
Careers-BMG Music, 1999/Floyd's Dream Music, 1999/Woolly Puddin'
  Music, 1999.
Introduced by the Dixie Chicks in the film and soundtrack album

Runaway Bride (Columbia, 99).Nominated for a Grammy Award, Best Country Song of the Year, 1999.

Reason to Believe
Words and music by Tim Hardin.
Hudson Bay Music, 1966.
Revived by Ron Sexsmith in the album *Bleecker Street: Greenwich Village in the '60s* (Astor Place, 99).

Red River
Words and music by Guy Clark.
EMI-April Music, 1999.
Revived by Guy Clark in the album *Cold Dog Soup* (Sugar Hill, 99).

Regrets
Words and music by Ben Folds.
Fresh Avery Music, 1999/Sony ATV Songs, 1999.
Introduced by Ben Folds Five in the album *The Unauthorized Biography of Reinhold Masoner* (550/Epic, 99).

Return of the Grievous Angel
Words and music by Gram Parsons and Thomas Brown.
Wait and See Music, 1974.
Revived by Lucinda Williams and David Crosby in the album *Return of the Grievous Angel: A Tribute to Gram Parsons* (Almo Sounds, 99).

Revolutionary Kind (English)
Words and music by Ian Ball.
WB Music, 1999.
Introduced by Gomez in the album *Liquid Skin* (Virgin, 99).

Right About Now (English)
Words and music by Ron Sexsmith.
Nomad-Noman Music, 1999/Warner-Tamerlane Music, 1999.
Introduced by Ron Sexsmith in the album *Whereabouts* (Interscope, 99).

Right Here, Right Now
Words and music by Cassandra Wilson and Marvin Sewell.
Llewes Music, 1999.
Introduced by Cassandra Wilson in the album *Travelling Miles* (Blue Note, 99).

Rock Is Dead
Words and music by Brian Warner, Stephen Bier, and Jeordie White.
Dinger & Ollie Music, 1998/Blood Heavy, 1998/DCLXVL Music, 1998/ Songs of Golgotha, 1998.
Revived by Marilyn Manson in the film and soundtrack album *The Matrix* (Maverick, 99).

Rock and Roll Hall of Lame
Words and music by Mojo Nixon.
Muffin Stuffin, 1999.
Introduced by Mojo Nixon in the album *The Real Sock Ray Blue*
  (Shanachie, 99).

Room at the Top
Words and music by Tom Petty.
Adria K Music, 1999/Wixen Music, 1999.
Introduced by Tom Petty in the album *Echo* (Warner Brothers, 99)
  .Nominated for a Grammy Award, Best Rock Song of the Year, 1999.

Running up That Hill (English)
Words and music by Kate Bush.
Screen Gems-EMI Music Inc., 1985.
Revived by the Baltimores in the album *I Wanna Be Kate* (Brown Star,
  99).

S

Satisfy
Words and music by Me Shell NdegeOcello and Federico Pena.
Nomad-Noman Music, 1999/Revolutionary Jazz Giant, 1999/Warner-
Tamerlane Music, 1999.
Introduced by Me Shell NdegeOcello in the album *Bitter* (Maverick,
99).

Satisfy You
Words and music by Sean Combs, Jeffrey Walker, R. Greene, Kelly
Price, Denzil Foster, Jay King, Thom McElroy, and Robert Kelly.
Justin Combs Music, 1999/EMI-April Music, 1999/Dub's World Music,
1999/Sony ATV Music, 1999/Thelma's Boi Music, 1999/Songs of
Universal, 1999/Price is Right Music, 1999/R. Kelly Music, 1999/
EMI-Blackwood Music Inc., 1999/Lehsem Music, 1999.
Best-selling record by Puff Daddy featuring R. Kelly in the album
Forever (Bad Boy/Arista, 99).

Save Me
Words and music by Aimee Mann.
Aimee Mann, 1999.
Introduced by Aimee Mann in the film and soundtrack album *Magnolia*
(Reprise, 99).Nominated for an Academy Award, Best Song of the
Year, 1999.

Scar Tissue
Words and music by Anthony Keidis, Flea (pseudonym for Michael
Balzary), John Frusciante, and Chad Smith.
Moebetoblame Music, 1999.
Best-selling record by Red Hot Chili Peppers in the album
Californication (Warner Brothers, 99).Won a Grammy Award for
Best Rock Song of the Year 1999.

The Secret of Life
Words and music by Gretchen Peters.
Sony ATV Cross Keys Publishing Co. Inc., 1999/Purple Crayon Music,

1999.
Best-selling record by Faith Hill in the album *Breathe* (Warner Brothers, 99).

17 Again (English)
Words and music by Annie Lennox and Dave Stewart.
Metcom Music, 1999/Logo Music, 1999.
Best-selling record by Eurythmics in the album *Peace* (Arista, 99).

Sexual Healing
Words and music by Marvin Gaye, David Ritz, and Odell Brown.
EMI-April Music, 1982/EMI-Blackwood Music Inc., 1982.
Revived by Michael Bolton in the album *Timeless (The Classics) Vol. 2* (Columbia, 99).

Sexx Laws
Words and music by Beck Hanson.
Cyanide Breathmint Music, 1998/BMG Music, 1999.
Introduced by Beck in the album *Midnight Vultures* (DGC, 98).

Shake Your Bon Bon (American-Puerto Rican)
English words and music by Robi Rosa, Jorge Noriega, and Desmond Child.
Desmophobia, 1999/Polygram Music Publishing Inc., 1999/A Phantom Vox Music, 1999/Warner-Tamerlane Music, 1999/Estefan Music, 1999.
Best-selling record by Ricky Martin in the album *Ricky Martin* (Sony, 99).

Shakin' All Over (English)
Words and music by Jonathan Kidd.
Mills Music Inc., 1960.
Revived by Iggy Pop in the album *Avenue B* (Virgin, 99).

She's All I Ever Had (Puerto Rican)
English words and music by Robi Rosa, Jorge Noriega, and Jon Secada.
A Phantom Vox Music, 1999/Warner-Tamerlane Music, 1999/Estefan Music, 1999/Foreign Imported, 1999.
Best-selling record by Ricky Martin in the album *Ricky Martin* (Sony, 99).

She's in Love
Words and music by Keith Stegall and Dan Hill.
EMI Tower Street Music, 1998/Little Cayman, 1998/If Dreams Had Wings, 1998/EMI-Blackwood Music Inc., 1998.
Best-selling record by Mark Wills in the album *Wish You Were Here* (Mercury, 98).

She's So High (Canadian)
Words and music by Tal Bachman.
Bachman & Sons Music, 1999/EMI-Blackwood Music Inc., 1999.
Best-selling record by Tal Bachman in the album *Tal Bachman* (Capitol, 99).

Silent Treatment
Words and music by Tarik Collins, Leonard Hubbard, Scott Storch, and Ahmir Thompson.
Careers-BMG Music.
Revived by the Roots in the album *The Roots Come Alive* (MCA, 99).

Single White Female
Words and music by Shaye Smith and Carolyn Johnson.
Blackmore Ave. Music, 1999/Mark Alan Springer Music, 1999/ Windswept Pacific, 1999/EMI-Blackwood Music Inc., 1999.
Best-selling record by Chely Wright in the album *Single White Female* (MCA Nashville, 99).

Sitting Home
Words and music by Jack Knight, Deric Angelettie, Garrett Blake, Kenneth Whitehead, and Errol Johnson.
Dakoda House Music, 1999/Justin Combs Music, 1999/EMI-April Music, 1999/Windswept Pacific, 1999/Polygram Music Publishing Inc., 1999/Motown Songs, 1999/Blake Karrington Music, 1999/Deric Angelettie Music, 1999.
Best-selling record by Total in the album *Kima, Keisha and Pam* (Bad Boy/Arista, 99).

Size of Our Love
Words and music by Carrie Brownstein.
Code Word Nemesis, Olympia, 1999.
Introduced by Sleater-Kinney in the album *The Hot Rock* (Kill Rock Stars, 99).

Sleepless Nights
Words and music by Felice Bryant and Boudleaux Bryant.
House of Bryant Publications, 1960.
Revived by Elvis Costello in the album *Return of the Grievous Angel: A Tribute to Gram Parsons* (Almo Sounds, 99).

Slowpoke
Words and music by Neil Young.
Silver Fiddle, 1999.
Introduced by Crosby, Stills, Nash & Young in the album *Looking Forward* (Reprise, 99).

Smoke Smoke Smoke That Cigarette
Words and music by Merle Travis and Tex Williams.

Unichappell Music Inc., 1947/Elvis Presley Music, 1947.
Revived by Marty Stuart in the film and soundtrack album *Hi Lo Country* (TVT Soundtrax, 99).

Smooth
Words and music by Itaal Shur and Rob Thomas.
Itall Shur Music, 1999/Bidnis Inc Music, 1999/EMI-Blackwood Music Inc., 1999/Warner-Tamerlane Music, 1999.
Best-selling record by Santana with Rob Thomas in the album *Supernatural* (Arista, 99).Won Grammy Awards.

So Anxious
Words and music by Stephen Garrett and Benjamin Bush.
Virginia Beach Music, 1999/Herbilicious Music, 1999/Blazalicious Music, 1999/Black Fountain, 1999/WB Music, 1999.
Best-selling record by Ginuwine in the album *100% Ginuwine* (550 Music, 99).

So Long Marianne (Canadian)
Words and music by Leonard Cohen.
Sony ATV Songs, 1967.
Revived by Suzanne Vega and John Cale in the album *Bleecker Street: Greenwich Village in the '60s* (Astor Place, 99).

Someday
Words and music by Sugar Ray and David Kahne.
Warner-Tamerlane Music, 1999/See Squared Music, 1999.
Best-selling record by Sugar Ray in the album *14:59* (Lava/Atlantic, 99).

Something Like That
Words and music by Rick Ferrell and Keith Follese.
We Make Music, 1999/Bud Dog Music, 1999/Follazoo Music, 1999/ Encore Entertainment, 1999/Mr. Noise Music, 1999.
Best-selling record by Tim McGraw in the album *A Place in the Sun* (Curb, 99).

Something to Live For
Words and music by Billy Strayhorn and Edward Kennedy "Duke" Ellington.
American Academy of Music, Inc., 1939.
Revived by Susannah McCorkle in the album *From Broken Hearts to Blue Skies* (Concord Jazz, 99).

Sometimes (Swedish)
English words and music by Joergen Elofsson and David Kreuger.
Zomba Music, 1998/Grantsville, 1998/BMG Scandinavia Music, 1998.
Best-selling record by Britney Spears in the album *..Baby One More Time* (Jive, 98).

Song for the Children
Words and music by Dan Bern.
Kababa Music, Los Angeles, 1999.
Introduced by Dan Bern on a limited edition sampler available only
through the Bronx, New York radio station WFUV-FM. This striking
song deals with the Columbine tragedy.

Southern Gul
Words and music by Erica Wright and Rahzel Brown.
Rahzel Music, 1999/Songs of Polygram, 1999.
Best-selling record by Rahzel and Erykah Badu in the album *Make the
Music 2000* (MCA, 99).

Space
Words and music by Ricky Ian Gordon and Tina Landau.
Introduced by Jeff McCarthy and Ensemble in the musical *Dreams True*.

Space Oddity (English)
Words and music by David Bowie.
Essex Music International, 1969.
Revived by Natalie Merchant in the album *Live in Concert* (Elektra, 99).

Special
Words and music by Duke Erickson, Shirley Manson, Steve Marker, and
Butch Vig.
Irving Music Inc., 1998/Vibe Crusher Music, 1998.
Best-selling record by Garbage in the album *Version 2.0* (Almo Sounds/
Interscope, 98).Nominated for a Grammy Award, Best Rock Song of
the Year, 1999.

Spend My Life with You
Words and music by Eric Benet, Demonte Posey, and George Nash.
India B Music, 1999/Songs of Polygram, 1999/Demontes Music, 1999/
Puddy Tat Music, 1999/Paradise Forever Music, 1999/Warner-
Tamerlane Music, 1999.
Best-selling record by Eric Benet featuring Tamia in the album *A Day
in the Life* (Warner Brothers, 99).

Spit on a Stranger
Words and music by Stephen Malkmus.
Treble Kicker Music, 1999.
Introduced by Pavement in the album *Terror Twilight* (Matador, 99).

Stand and Be Counted
Words and music by David Crosby and James Raymond.
Stay Straight Music, 1999/Proudfoot Music, 1999.
Introduced by Crosby, Stills, Nash & Young in the album *Looking
Forward* (Reprise, 99).

Stand Beside Me
Words and music by Stephen Davis.
Hamstein Cumberland, Nashville, 1998/Red Brazos, 1998.
Best-selling record by Jo Dee Messina in the album *I'm Alright* (Curb, 98).

Stars All Seem to Weep (Canadian)
Words and music by Beth Orton.
EMI-Blackwood Music Inc., 1999.
Introduced by Beth Orton in the album *Central Reservation* (DeConstruction/Arista, 99).

Start Together
Words and music by Carrie Brownstein.
Code Word Nemesis, Olympia, 1999.
Introduced by Sleater-Kinney in the album *The Hot Rock* (Kill Rock Stars, 99).

Stay the Night
Words and music by Tony Isaac, Marques Houston, Jerome Jones, and Tony Oliver.
Blue Khakis Music, 1999/Young Fiano Music, 1999/Demolition Man Music, 1999/T. Scott Style Music, 1999/Put It Down Music, 1999.
Best-selling record by Joey McIntyre in the album *Stay the Same* (C2, 99).

Stay the Same
Words and music by Joe McIntyre and Joseph Carrier.
Cristjen Music, 1999/WB Music, 1999.
Best-selling record by Joey McIntyre in the album *Stay the Same* (C2, 99).

Staying Power
Words and music by Joey Paschal and Rory Holmes.
Seven Music, 1999.
Best-selling record by Barry White in the album *Staying Power* (Private, 99).

Steal My Sunshine
Words and music by Marc Castanzo and Gregg Diamond.
Buddah Music Inc., 1999/Big Meanie Music, 1999/MRI Music, 1999/ EMI-April Music, 1999/Hope Chest Music, 1999/BMG Music, 1999/ EMI U Catalogue, 1999.
Introduced by Len in the film and soundtrack album *Go* (Sony, 99).

A Step Too Far (English)
Words and music by Elton John and Tim Rice.
Happenstance Music, 1999/Sixty Four Square Music, 1999/Wonderland Music, 1999.

Best-selling record by Elton John/Heather Hadley/Sherie Scott in the album *Elton John's Aida* (Rocket/Mercury, 99).

Stolen Car (Canadian)
Words and music by Beth Orton, Ted Barnes, William Blanchard, and Sean Read.
EMI-Blackwood Music Inc., 1999/Heavenly Sounds Music, 1999/ Warner-Tamerlane Music, 1999.
Introduced by Beth Orton in the album *Central Reservation* (DeConstruction/Arista, 99).

Stranger on the Shore (English)
Words and music by Acker Bilk (pseudonym for Bernard Stanley Bilk) and Robert Mellin.
Screen Gems-EMI Music Inc., 1961.
Revived by Kenny G in the album *Songs in the Key of G* (Arista, 99).

Strangers Like Me (English)
Words and music by Phil Collins.
Edgar Rice Burroughs Music, 1999/Walt Disney Music, 1999.
Introduced by Phil Collins in the film and soundtrack album *Tarzan* (Walt Disney/Hollywood, 99).

Summer Girls
Words and music by Rich Cronin, Brad Young, and Dow Brain.
Trans Continental Music, 1999.
Best-selling record by LFO in the album *LFO* (LogicArista, 99).

Summer Teeth
Words and music by Jeff Tweedy, Jay Bennett, John Stirratt, and Ken Coomer.
Words Ampersand Music, 1999/Warner-Tamerlane Music, 1999/You Want a Piece of This Music, 1999/Bug Music, 1999/Poeyfarre Music, 1999/Ft. Toe Music, 1999.
Introduced by Wilco in the album *Summer Teeth* (Reprise, 99).

Surrender (English)
Words and music by Andrew Lloyd Webber, Donald Black, and James Hampton Christopher.
Songs of Polygram, 1990.
Revived by Betty Buckley in the album *Betty Buckley's Broadway* (Sterling, 99). From the musical Sunset Boulevard.

Sweet Child of Mine
Words and music by Axl Rose, Slash (pseudonym for Saul Hudson), Izzy Stradlin, Stephen Adler, and Duff McKagen.
Guns N' Roses Music, 1987.
Revived by Sheryl Crow in the film and soundtrack album *Big Daddy*

(American/Sony Music, 99). Also Revived by Luna in the album *The Days of Our Nights* (Jericho, 99).

Sweet Lady
Words and music by Dallas Austin, Troy Taylor, and Charles Farrar.
Kharatroy Music, 1999/B. Black Music, 1999/Naked Under My Clothes
    Music, 1999/Chrysalis Music Group, 1999/WB Music, 1999.
Best-selling record by Tyrese in the album *Tyrese* (RCA, 98).

T

Take Me There
Words and music by Teddy Riley, Tamara Savage, Madeline Nelson, Mason Betha, and Michael Foster.
Zomba Music, 1999/EMI-April Music, 1999/Marshall Music, 1999/ Justin Combs Music, 1999/Mason Betha Music, 1999/Music by Nickelodean, 1999/Tunes by Nickelodean, 1999.
Best-selling record by Blacksheep and Mya featuring Blinky Blink in the album *Finally* (Interscope, 99).

Take a Picture
Words and music by Richard Patrick.
EMI-April Music, 1999/Happy Ditties from Paradise, 1999.
Best-selling record by Filter in the album *Title of Record* (Reprise, 99).

Taking Everything
Words and music by Gerald Levert, Darrell Allamby, Lincoln Browder, and Antoinette Roberson.
2000 Watts Music, Newark, 1998/Divided, 1998/Zomba Music, 1998/WB Music, 1998/Toni Robi Music, 1998.
Best-selling record by Gerard Levert in the album *Love and Consequences* (EastWest, 98).

Tea Song
Words and music by Peter Stampfel and Michael Hurley.
Storm King Music Inc., 1999.
Revived by the Holy Modal Rounders in the album *Too Much Fun* (Rounder, 99).

Tear Me Down
Words and music by Stephen Schwartz.
So Do My Songs, 1998.
Revived by John Cameron Mitchell in the original cast album *Hedwig and the Angry Inch* (Atlantic, 99).

Tears on My Pillow
Words and music by Sylvester Bradford and Al Lewis.
Gladys Music, 1958/Sovereign Music Corp., 1958.
Revived by K-Ci & JoJo in the TV show and soundtrack album *Shake, Rattle & Roll* (MCA, 99).

Tell Me It's Real
Words and music by Cedric Hailey and Rory Bennett.
Cord Kayla Music, 1999/Hee Bee Doinit, 1999/Big Prod Music, 1999/ EMI-April Music, 1999/WB Music, 1999.
Best-selling record by K-Ci & JoJo in the album *It's Real* (MCA, 99).

Thank You (Falletten Me Be Myself Again)
Words and music by Sylvester Stewart.
Warner-Tamerlane Music, 1970.
Revived by Barry White in the film and soundtrack album *EDTV* (Reprise, 99).

That Don't Impress Me Much
Words and music by Shania Twain and Robert John Lange.
Polygram Music Publishing Inc., 1998/Zomba Music, 1998/Loon Echo Music, 1998.
Best-selling record by Shania Twain in the album *Come on Over* (Mercury Nashville, 98).

That's the Way It Is (German)
English words and music by Max Martin, Kristian Lundin, and Andreas Carlsson.
Grantsville, 1999/Zomba Music, 1999.
Introduced by Celine Dion in the album *All the Way..A Decade of Song* (550 Music, 99).

That's the Way Love Goes
Words and music by Lefty Frizell and Sanger Shafer.
Acuff Rose Music, 1974.
Revived by Merle Haggard and Jewel in the album *For the Record* (BNA, 99).

That's What Makes You Strong (Canadian)
Words and music by Jesse Winchester.
WB Music, 1999/Fourth Floor Music Inc., 1999.
Introduced by Jesse Winchester in the album *Gentleman of Leisure* (Sugar Hill, 99).

Then the Morning Comes
Words and music by Gregory Camp and John Barry.
Squish Moth Music, 1999/Warner-Tamerlane Music, 1999/EMI Unart Music, 1999.

Best-selling record by Smash Mouth in the album *Astro Lounge*
(Interscope, 99).

There She Goes (English)
Words and music by Lee Anthony Mavers.
Go! Discs Ltd., England, 1982.
Best-selling record by Sixpence None the Richer in the album *Sixpence
None the Richer* (Squint/Elektra, 99).

These Are the Times
Words and music by Babyface (pseudonym for Kenneth Edmunds) and
Damon Thomas.
Ecaf Music, 1998/Demis Music, 1998/EMI-April Music, 1998/EZ
Music, 1998/Sony ATV Songs, 1998.
Best-selling record by Dru Hill the album *Enter the Dru* (Elektra, 98).

They Were You
Words and music by Tom Jones and Harvey Schmidt.
Chappell & Co., Inc., 1960.
Revived by Barbara Cook in the album *The Championship Season*
(DRG, 99).

This Friendly World
Words and music by Ken Darby.
Miller Music Corp., 1959.
Revived by R.E.M. and Jim Carrey in the film and soundtrack album
Man on the Moon (Warner Brothers/Jersey, 99). Introduced by Fabian
in the movie Hound Dog Man.

This Is Your Time
Words and music by Michael W. Smith and Wesley King.
Sparrow Song Music, 1999/Uncle Ivan Music, 1999.
Best-selling record by Michael W. Smith in the album *This Is Your
Time* (Reunion, 99). Inspired by the shootings at Columbine High
School and nominated for several Dove awards.

A Thousand Years (English)
Words and music by Sting (pseudonym for Gordon Sumner) and Kipper.
EMI-Blackwood Music Inc., 1999/Magnetic Music Publishing Co.,
1999.
Introduced by Sting in the album *Brand New Day* (A&M, 99).

Thursday's Child (English)
Words and music by David Bowie.
Jones Music America, 1999.
Introduced by David Bowie in the album *Hours* (Virgin, 99).

The Time of Your Life
Words and music by Randy Newman.

Wonderland Music, 1999.
Introduced by Randy Newman in the film and soundtrack album *A Bug's Life* (Disney, 99).Nominated for a Grammy Award, Best Song Written for a Movie, 1999.

Tionne's Song
Words and music by Tionne Watkins.
Grung Girl Music, 1999.
Introduced by Tionne "T-Boz" Watkins in the audio book *Thoughts* (Harper, 99).

To Live Is to Fly
Words and music by Townes Van Zandt.
Columbine Music Inc., 1972.
Revived by Townes Van Zandt in the album *A Far Cry from Dead* (Arista Austin, 99).

To Sir with Love (English)
Words and music by Don Black and Mark London.
Screen Gems-EMI Music Inc., 1967.
Revived by Vonda Shepherd and Al Green in the TV show and soundtrack album *Heart and Soul: New Songs from Ally McBeal, Featuring Vonda Shepherd* (Epic/550, 99).

Tonight the Heartache's on Me
Words and music by Mary Francis, Johnny Macrae, and Bob Morrison.
Music City Music, 1999/EMI-April Music, 1999/Southern Days Music, 1999.
Best-selling record by the Dixie Chicks in the album *Fly* (Monument, 99).

Tonya's Twirls
Words and music by Loudon Wainwright.
Snowden Music, 1999.
Introduced by Loudon Wainwright in the album *Social Studies* (Hannibal/Rykodisc, 99). This song chronicles the travails of the notorious figure skater Tonya Harding.

Too Fast for Love
Words and music by Nikki Sixx.
WB Music, 1983.
Revived by the Donnas in the album *Get Skintight* (Lookout, 99).

Troubled Times
Words and music by Chris Collingwood and Adam Schlesinger.
Monkey Demon Music, 1999/Awkward Paws Music, 1999/EMI Music Publishing, 1999.
Introduced by Fountains of Wayne in the album *Utopia Parkway* (Atlantic, 99).

Turn Your Lights down Low
Words and music by Bob Marley.
BMG Music, 1977.
Revived by Lauryn Hill and Bob Marley in the film and soundtrack
    album *The Best Man* (Columbia/Sony Music Soundtrax, 99).

24/7
Words and music by Angelo Ray, David Scott, and Anthony Smith.
Cross Town Music, 1999.
Best-selling record by Kevon Edmunds in the album *24/7* (RCA, 99).

Two Teardrops
Words and music by Bill Anderson and Steve Wariner.
Mr. Bubba Music, 1999/Sony ATV Tree Publishing, 1999/Steve
    Wariner, 1999.
Best-selling record by Steve Wariner in the album *Two Teardrops*
    (Capitol, 99).Nominated for a Grammy Award, Best Country Song of
    the Year, 1999.

U

U Know What's Up
Words and music by Delvis Damon, Edward Ferrell, Clifton Lighty,
  Darren Lighty, Anthony Hamilton, and Balewa Muhammed.
Eddie F. Music, 1999/Do What I Gotta Music, 1999/WB Music, 1999/
  Balewa Music, 1999/MCA Music, 1999/Anthony C. Music, 1999/
  Rassmysteria Music, 1999/Rusty Knuckles Music, 1999.
Best-selling record by Donell Jones in the album *Where I Wanna Be*
  (LaFace/Arista, 99).

Unbelievable
Words and music by Al Anderson and Jeffrey Steele.
Al Andersongs, Nashville, 1998/Mighty Nice Music, 1998/My Life's
  Work Music, 1998/EMI-Full Keel Music, 1998/EMI-Songs of
  Windswept Pacific, 1998/Yellow Desert Music, 1998.
Best-selling record by Diamond Rio in the album *Unbelievable* (Arista
  Nashville, 98).

Unforgetful You
Words and music by Dan Haseltine, Matt Odmark, Steve Mason, and
  Charlie Lowell.
Brentwood Music, Brentwood, 1999/Bridge Building Music, 1999/Pogo
  Stick Music, 1999.
Introduced by Jars of Clay in the film and soundtrack album *Drive Me
  Crazy* (Jive, 99). Also featured on the album *If I Left the Zoo*
  (Essential/Silvertone, 99).

Unpretty
Words and music by Dallas Austin and Tionne Watkins.
Cyptron Music, 1999/Grung Girl Music, 1999/EMI-Blackwood Music
  Inc., 1999.
Best-selling record by TLC in the album *Fan Mail* (LaFace/Arista, 99)
  .Nominated for a Grammy Award, Best Song of the Year, 1999.

Up Up Up Up Up Up
Words and music by Ani DiFranco.

Righteous Babe Music, Buffalo, 1999.
Introduced by Ani DiFranco in the album *Up Up Up Up Up Up* (Righteous Babe, 99).

V

Via Chicago
Words and music by Jeff Tweedy, Jay Bennett, John Stirratt, and Ken Coomer.
Words Ampersand Music, 1999/Warner-Tamerlane Music, 1999/You Want a Piece of This Music, 1999/Bug Music, 1999/Poeyfarre Music, 1999/Ft. Toe Music, 1999.
Introduced by Wilco in the album *Summer Teeth* (Reprise, 99).

Vida (Life)
Words and music by Ruben Blades.
Ruben Blades Music, 1999.
Introduced by Ruben Blades in the album *Tiempos* (Sony Discos, 99).

Vivrant Thing
Words and music by Kamaal Fareed.
Zomba Music, 1999/Jazz Merchant Music, 1999.
Best-selling record by Q-Tip in the album *Amplified* (Violator/Def Jam, 99).

W

Waitin' for a Superman
Words and music by Wayne Coyne, Steven Drozd, and Michael Ivins.
Lovely Sorts of Death Music, 1999/EMI-Blackwood Music Inc., 1999.
Introduced by the Flaming Lips in the album *The Soft Bulletin* (Warner Brothers, 99).

Waiting for Tonight
Words and music by Maria Abraham, Philip Temple, and Michael Garvin.
Sweet Woo Music, 1999/Annotation Music, 1999/Connotation Music, 1999/Michael Garvin Music, 1999/Denonation Music, 1999/WB Music, 1999/Warner-Tamerlane Music, 1999/RPM Music, 1999.
Best-selling record by Jennifer Lopez in the album *On the 6* (Work, 99).

Way Back to Paradise
Words and music by Robert John LaChuisa.
Revived by Audra Mcdonald in the operetta *Maria Christine*.

We Can't Be Friends
Words and music by Shep Crawford and J. Russell.
Shep Shep Music, 1998/Hudson Jordan, 1998/Wixen Music, 1998/Famous Music Corp., 1998.
Best-selling record by Deborah Cox with RL in the album *One Wish* (Arista, 98).

We Like to Party (Norwegian)
English words and music by Danski and D. J. Delmundo.
Peermusic Ltd., 1999.
Best-selling record by Vengaboys in the album *The Party Album* (Groovilicious/Strictly Rhythm, 99).

We Will Always Walk Together
Words and music by Ricky Ian Gordon and Tina Landau.
Introduced by Arnel Jenkins in the musical *Dreams True* (, 99).

Weird
Words and music by Lou Barlow.
Loobiecore Music, 1999.
Introduced by Sebadoh in the album *The Sebadoh* (Sub Pop/Sire, 99).

We're All Alone
Words and music by William Scaggs.
Boz Scaggs Music, 1976.
Revived by Reba McEntire in the album *So Good Together* (MCA
 Nashville, 99).

We're in This Together
Words and music by Trent Reznor.
TVT, NYC, 1999/Kid Capri, 1999.
Best-selling record by Nine Inch Nails in the album *The Fragile*
 (Nothing/Interscope, 99).

What Do You Say
Words and music by Michael Dulaney and Neil Thrasher.
Michael Dulaney Music, 1999/Dulaney House Music, 1999/Ensign
 Music, 1999/Major Bob Music, 1999.
Best-selling record by Reba McEntire in the album *So Good Together*
 (MCA Nashville, 99).

What Do You Say to That
Words and music by Jim Lauderdale and Melba Montgomery.
Laudersongs, 1999/Yah Yah Music, 1999/Mighty Nice Music, 1999/
 Caroljac Music, 1999/CMI America, 1999.
Best-selling record by George Strait in the album *Always Never the
 Same* (MCA Nashville, 99).

What a Girl Wants
Words and music by Shelly Peiken and Guy Roche.
Warner-Tamerlane Music, 1999/Hidden Pun Music, 1999/Sushi Too
 Music, 1999/Manuiti LA Music, 1999.
Best-selling record by Christina Aguilera in the album *Christina
 Aguilera* (RCA, 99).

What It's Like
Words and music by Everlast Schrody.
Slack A. D. Music, 1999/T-Boy Music Publishing Co., Inc., 1999.
Best-selling record by Everlast in the album *Whitey Ford Sings the
 Blues* (Tommy Boy, 98).

What Ya Want
Words and music by Kasseem Dean and Eve Jeffers.
Blondie Rockwell Music, 1999/Swizz Beats Music, 1999/Dead Game
 Music, 1999.

Best-selling record by Eve & Nokio in the album *Let There Be..Eve-Ruff Ryders' First Lady* (Ruff Ryders/Interscope, 99).

What You Don't Know About Women
Words and music by Cy Coleman and David Zippel.
Notable Music Co., Inc., 1989.
Revived by Emily Skinner and Alice Ripley in the album *Unsuspecting Hearts* (Varese Sarabande, 99). Originated in musical City of Angels.

Whatever You Say
Words and music by Anthony Martin and Edward Hill.
Hamstein Cumberland, Nashville, 1999/Baby Mae Music, Austin, 1999/ Music Hill Music, Nashville/New Haven Music, 1999.
Best-selling record by Martina McBride in the album *Emotion* (RCA Nashville, 99).

What's He Building
Words and music by Tom Waits.
Jalma Music, 1999.
Introduced by Tom Waits in the album *Mule Variations* (Epitaph, 99).

What's It Gonna Be
Words and music by Rashad Smith, Darrell Allamby, and Antoinette Roberson.
2000 Watts Music, Newark, 1999/T'Ziah's Music, 1999/Toni Robi Music, 1999/Warner-Tamerlane Music, 1999/WB Music, 1999.
Best-selling record by Busta Rhymes featuring Janet Jackson in the album *E.L.E. Extinction Level Event* (Flipmode/Elektra, 99).

What's My Age Again
Words and music by Tom DeLange and Mark Hopkins.
EMI-April Music, 1999/Fun with Goats Music, 1999.
Best-selling record by Blink 182 in the album *Enema of the State* (MCA, 99).

When I Close My Eyes
Words and music by Warryn Campbell and Tamara Savage.
EMI-April Music, 1999.
Best-selling record by Shanice in the album *Shanice* (Laface/Arista, 99).

When I Look in Your Eyes (English)
Words and music by Leslie Bricusse.
Mint Condition Music, 1967.
Revived by Diana Krall in the album *When I Look in Your Eyes* (Verve, 99). From the movie Dr. Doolittle.

When I Said I Do
Words and music by Clint Black.
Blackened Music, 1999.

Best-selling record by Clint Black in the album *D'Lectrified* (RCA Nashville, 99).

When the Leaves Come Falling Down (English)
Words and music by Van Morrison.
Songs of Polygram, 1999.
Introduced by Van Morrison in the album *Back on Top* (Pointblank, 99).

When She Loved Me
Words and music by Randy Newman.
Wonderland Music, 1999.
Introduced by Sarah McLachlan in the film and soundtrack album *Toy Story II* (Walt Disney, 99).Nominated for an Academy Award, Best Song of the Year, 1999.

When a Woman's Fed Up
Words and music by Robert Kelly.
Zomba Music, 1999/R. Kelly Music, 1999.
Best-selling record by R. Kelly in the album *R.* (Jive, 98).

When You Believe (Prince of Egypt)
Words and music by Stephen Schwartz and Babyface (pseudonym for Kenny Edmunds).
Cherry Lane Music Co., 1998/Cherry River Music Co., 1998.
Best-selling record by Whitney Houston and Mariah Carey in the film and soundtrack album *Prince of Egypt* (DreamWorks, 98).Nominated for a Grammy Award, Best Song Written for a Movie, 1999.

Where My Girls At
Words and music by Missy Elliott, Rapture Stewart, and Eric Seats.
Mass Confusion Music, 1999/Virginia Beach Music, 1999/WB Music, 1999.
Best-selling record by 702 in the album *702* (Motown, 99).

Where Were You on Our Wedding Day
Words and music by Harold Logan, Lloyd Price, and John Patton.
Duchess Music Corp., 1959.
Revived by Billy Joel in the film and soundtrack album *Runaway Bride* (Columbia, 99).

Whiskey in the Jar (Irish)
Words and music by Traditional.
Best-selling record by Metallica in the album *Garage, Inc.* (Elektra, 99).

Who Dat
Words and music by Christopher Stewart, J. T. Money, Tony Mercedes, Tonya Johnston, Nkhereanye Thabigo, and Diandra Davis.
Famous Music Corp., 1999/Tunes on the Verge of Insanity, 1999/Mo Better Grooves Music, 1999/Rufftown Music, 1999/Tony Mercedes

Music, 1999/Honey from Missouri Music, 1999/Hit Co. South, 1999/
Tabulous Music, 1999/Money Man Music, 1999/Pepper Drive Music,
1999.
Best-selling record by J. T. Money in the album *Pimpin' on Wax* (Tony
Mercedes/Freeworld/Priority, 99).

Why Don't You Get a Job
Words and music by Bryan Holland.
Underachiever Music, Calabasas, 1999/Wixen Music, 1999.
Best-selling record by the Offspring in the album *Americana* (Columbia,
99).

Why I'm Here
Words and music by Doug Eldridge, Thomas Flowers, Ric Ivanisevich,
and Fred Jr. Nelson.
Oleander Noise Music, 1999/Songs of Universal, 1999.
Best-selling record by Oleander in the album *February Sun* (Republic/
Universal, 99).

Why Should I Care
Words and music by Clint Eastwood, Carole Bayer Sager, and Linda
Thompson.
E-Forty Music, 1999/Brandon & Brody Music, 1999/Warner-Tamerlane
Music, 1999.
Introduced by Diana Krall in the film and soundtrack album *True Crime*
(Verve, 99).

Wild Wild West
Words and music by Will Smith, Stevie Wonder, Moe Dewese, and
Robert Fusari.
Treyball Music, 1999/EMI-April Music, 1999/Zomba Music, 1999/Black
Bull Music, 1999.
Best-selling record by Will Smith featuring Dru Hill and Kool Moe Dee
in the film and soundtrack album *Wild Wild West* (Columbia, 99).

Will 2K
Words and music by Will Smith, Rory Bennett, Cedric Hailey, Bobby
Robinson, and the Clash.
Nineden, Ltd., London, England, 1999/Treyball Music, 1999/Love N
Loyalty Music, 1999/O' Brook Music, 1999/Bobby Robinson Music,
1999/Hee Bee Doinit, 1999/EMI-Virgin, 1999/EMI-April Music,
1999.
Best-selling record by Will Smith featuring K-Ci in the album
Willennium (Columbia, 99).

Wise Up
Words and music by Aimee Mann.
Aimee Mann, 1999.

Performed by Aimee Mann and cast in the film and soundtrack album *Magnolia* (Reprise, 99).

Wish You Were Here
Words and music by Skip Ewing, Bill Anderson, and Debbie Moore.
Sony ATV Tree Publishing, 1998/Mr. Bubba Music, 1998/Belton Uncle Music, 1998/Acuff Rose Music, 1998.
Best-selling record by Mark Wills in the album *Wish You Were Here* (Mercury Nashville, 98).

With You
Words and music by Matt Hendricks and Robin Lee Bruce.
WB Music, 1999/Dreamin' Upstream Music, 1999/Big Red Tractor Music, 1999.
Best-selling record by Lila McCann in the album *Something in the Air* (Asylum, 99).

Woke up This Morning
Words and music by Larry Love and Spirit.
Revived by A3 in the TV show and soundtrack album *The Sopranos* (Columbia, 99).

The World Is Not Enough
Words and music by David Arnold and Don Black.
United Lion Music Inc., 1999.
Introduced by Garbage in the film and soundtrack album *The World Is Not Enough* (MCA, 99).

Write This Down
Words and music by Dana Hunt and Kent Robbins.
Neon Sky Music, 1999/Irving Music Inc., 1999/Colter Bay Music, 1999.
Best-selling record by George Strait in the album *Always Never the Same* (MCA Nashville, 99).

Written in the Stars (English)
Words and music by Elton John and Tim Rice.
Happenstance Music, 1999/Sixty Four Square Music, 1999/Wonderland Music, 1999.
Best-selling record by Elton John and LeAnn Rimes in the album *Elton John's Aida* (Curb/Rocket, 99).

Wrong Again
Words and music by Thomas James and Cynthia Weil.
Still Working for the Man Music, 1999/Dyad Music, Ltd., 1999.
Best-selling record by Martina McBride in the album *Emotion* (RCA Nashville, 98).

Wrong Night
Words and music by Josh Leo and Rick Bowles.

Dead Solid Perfect Music, 1999/Hellmaymen, 1999/Warner-Tamerlane Music, 1999/Starstruck Writers Group, 1999.
Best-selling record by Reba McEntire in the album *Secret of Giving* (MCA Nashville, 99).

Y

You
Words and music by Carl Roland and Jesse Powell.
EMI-April Music, 1999/Ya Digg Music, 1999/Chrysalis Music Group,
1999/To the Third Power Music, 1999.
Best-selling record by Jesse Powell in the album *'Bout It* (Silas/MCA,
99).

You Don't Miss Your Water
Words and music by William Bell.
Irving Music Inc., 1961.
Revived by Harry Dean Stanton in the album *Rx* (Remedy, 99).

You Drive Me Crazy (Swedish)
English words and music by Joergen Elofsson, Per Magnusson, David
Kreuger, and Max Martin.
BMG Scandinavia Music, 1998/Zomba Music, 1998/Grantsville, 1998/
Careers-BMG Music, 1998.
Best-selling record by Britney Spears in the film and soundtrack album
Drive Me Crazy (Jive, 98).

You Get What You Give
Words and music by Greg Alexander and Rick Nowels.
Grosse Point Harlem Music, 1998/Streamline Moderne, 1998.
Best-selling record by New Radicals in the album *Maybe You've Been
Brainwashed Too* (MCA, 98).

You Give Me Love
Words and music by Matraca Berg, Jim Photoglo, and Harry Stinson.
Maria Belle, 1998/Otherwise, 1998/Sony ATV Tree Publishing, 1998/
Warner-Tamerlane Music, 1998.
Revived by by Faith Hill as the closing song for the final episode of the
TV series *Mad About You* (99).

You Got Me
Words and music by Tarik Trotter, Ahmir Thompson, Jill Scott, and

Scott Storch.
Careers-BMG Music, 1999.
Best-selling record by the Roots, featuring Erykah Badu in the album
Things Fall Apart (MCA, 99).

You Had Me from Hello
Words and music by Kenny Chesney and Skip Ewing.
Acuff Rose Music, 1999.
Best-selling record by Kenny Chesney in the album *Everywhere We Go*
(BNA, 99).

You Wanted More
Words and music by Emerson Hart, Dan Lavery, and Jeff Russo.
Crazy Owl Music, 1999/EMI-Blackwood Music Inc., 1999/Unconcerned
Music, 1999.
Best-selling record by Tonic in the soundtrack album from the film
American Pie (Universal, 99).

You Were Mine
Words and music by Emily Erwin and Martie Seidel.
Woolly Puddin' Music, 1999/Bug Music, 1999.
Best-selling record by Dixie Chicks in the album *Fly* (Monument, 98).

You Won't Ever Be Lonely
Words and music by Andy Griggs and William Jones.
Sony ATV Tree Publishing, 1999/Mo Fuzzy Dice Music, 1999/Famous
Music Corp., 1999.
Best-selling record by Andy Griggs in the album *You Won't Ever Be
Lonely* (RCA Nashville, 99).

You'll Be in My Heart
Words and music by Phil Collins.
Edgar Rice Burroughs Music, 1999/Walt Disney Music, 1999.
Best-selling record by Phil Collins in the album *Tarzan* (Walt Disney/
Hollywood, 99).Won an Academy Award for Best Song of the Year
1999. Nominated for a Grammy Award, Best Song Written for a
Movie, 1999.

Your Child
Words and music by Gerald Isaac.
Groove Child Music, 1999/Songs of Polygram, 1999.
Introduced by Mary J. Blige in the album *Mary* (MCA, 99).

Your Dictionary (English)
Words and music by Andy Partridge.
EMI-Virgin, 1999.
Introduced by XTC in the album *Apple Venus Volume 1* (Idea/TVT, 99).

You're Older Than You've Ever Been
Words and music by Loudon Wainwright.
Snowden Music, 1999.
Introduced by Loudon Wainwright on the TV show *Nightline*. Featured
   in the album *Social Studies* (Hannibal/Rykodisco, 99).

You've Got a Way
Words and music by Shania Twain and Robert John Lange.
Songs of Polygram, 1999/Zomba Music, 1999/Loon Echo Music, 1999.
Revived by Shania Twain in the film and soundtrack album *Nottinghill*
   (Mercury, 99).Nominated for a Grammy Award, Best Song of the
   Year, 1999.

Lyricists & Composers Index

Abraham, Maria
  Waiting for Tonight
Ackerman, Tracey
  C'est La Vie
Adams, Terry
  Pain
Adler, Stephen
  Sweet Child of Mine
Alexander, Greg
  You Get What You Give
Allamby, Darrell
  If You (Lovin' Me)
  Taking Everything
  What's It Gonna Be
Amos, Tori
  Bliss
  1000 Oceans
Andersen, Eric
  Rain Falls down in Amsterdam
Anderson, Al
  Big Deal
  Powerful Thing
  Unbelievable
Anderson, Bill
  Two Teardrops
  Wish You Were Here
Angelettie, Deric
  Sitting Home
Anthony, Mark
  I Need to Know
Apple, Fiona
  Fast as You Can
  I Know

On the Bound
Paper Bag
April, Johnny
  Mudshovel
Arnaou, Lindsay
  C'est La Vie
Arnold, David
  The World Is Not Enough
Atkins, Jeffrey
  Holla Holla
Austin, Dallas
  Sweet Lady
  Unpretty
Austin, Johnta
  Get Gone
Austin, Sherrie
  Never Been Kissed
Austin, Simon
  David Duchovny
Baby
  Bling Bling
Babyface
  My First Night with You
  Never Gonna Let You Go
  These Are the Times
  When You Believe (Prince of Egypt)
Bachman, Randy
  American Woman
Bachman, Tal
  She's So High
Baker, Bonnie
  Ordinary Life

Lyricists & Composers Index

Baldes, Kevin
  My Own Worst Enemy
Ball, Ian
  Revolutionary Kind
Balzary, Michael *see* Flea
Barlow, Lou
  My Ritual
  Weird
Barnes, Max T.
  A Night to Remember
Barnes, Samuel
  Did You Ever Think
  Hold Me
Barnes, Ted
  Stolen Car
Barnhill, Greg
  Never Been Kissed
Barrier, Eric
  Re-Arranged
Barry, John
  Millennium
  Then the Morning Comes
Barry, Paul
  Bailamos
  Believe
Bean, Richard
  Every Morning
Beckerman, Danny
  Just Wave Hello
Beckwith, Kilu
  I've Committed Murder
Bega, Lou
  Mambo No. 5 (A Little Bit of..)
Bell, William
  You Don't Miss Your Water
Benbow, D.
  Get It on Tonite
Benet, Eric
  Spend My Life with You
Bennett, Jay
  Can't Stand It
  Summer Teeth
  Via Chicago
Bennett, Rory
  Tell Me It's Real
  Will 2K
Bentley, Stephanie
  Breathe

Berg, Matraca
  You Give Me Love
Bergman, Alan
  Ex-Factor
Bergman, Marilyn
  Ex-Factor
Bern, Dan
  Joe van Gogh
  Krautmeyer
  Song for the Children
Betha, Mason
  Take Me There
Biancaniello, L.
  I Wanna Love You Forever
Bier, Stephen
  Rock Is Dead
Bilk, Acker
  Stranger on the Shore
Bilk, Bernard Stanley *see* Bilk, Acker
Black, Clint
  When I Said I Do
Black, Don
  New Ways to Dream
  To Sir with Love
  The World Is Not Enough
Black, Donald
  Surrender
Blades, Ruben
  Dia a Dia (Every Day)
  Vida (Life)
Blake, Garrett
  Sitting Home
Blanchard, William
  Stolen Car
Bobbit, Charles
  Re-Arranged
Bono
  Conversation on a Barstool
Borland, Wesley
  Nookie
  Re-Arranged
Bowie, David
  Space Oddity
  Thursday's Child
Bowles, Rick
  Wrong Night
Boyd, Jason, Jr.
  Anywhere

Bradford, Sylvester
  Tears on My Pillow
Brain, Dow
  Girl on TV
  Summer Girls
Brannigan, Martin
  C'est La Vie
Bricusse, Leslie
  Millennium
  When I Look in Your Eyes
Briggs, Kevin
  Bills Bills Bills
  Bug a Boo
  No Pigeons
  No Scrubs
Brooke, Jonatha
  Is This All
Browder, Lincoln
  If You (Lovin' Me)
  Taking Everything
Brown, James
  Re-Arranged
Brown, Jason Robert
  All the Wasted Time
  It's Not over Yet
Brown, Odell
  Sexual Healing
Brown, Rahzel
  Southern Gul
Brown, Thomas
  Return of the Grievous Angel
Brown, Vinnie
  Jamboree
Browne, Jackson
  For a Dancer
Brownstein, Carrie
  Size of Our Love
  Start Together
Bruce, Robin Lee
  With You
Bryan
  No Pigeons
Bryant, Boudleaux
  Sleepless Nights
Bryant, Felice
  Sleepless Nights
Bryson, David
  Hanging Around

Bryson, Peabo
  Did You Ever Know
Buck, Peter
  At My Most Beautiful
  The Great Beyond
Buckcherry
  For the Movies
  Lit Up
Bullens, Cindy
  Better Than I've Ever Been
Bullock, Craig
  Every Morning
Burruss, Kandi
  Bills Bills Bills
  Bug a Boo
  4, 5, 6
  No Pigeons
  No Scrubs
Bush, Benjamin
  So Anxious
Bush, Kate
  Running up That Hill
Byrd, Bobby
  Re-Arranged
Cadogan, Kevin
  New Girl
Calhoun, Charles
  Losing Hand
Camp, Gregory
  All Star
  Then the Morning Comes
Campbell, Warryn
  When I Close My Eyes
Cantrell, Jerry
  Get Born Again
Carey, Mariah
  Can't Take That Away (Mariah's
    Theme)
  Heartbreaker
Carlsson, Andreas
  I Want It That Way
  That's the Way It Is
Carpenter, Mary Chapin
  Almost Home
Carrier, Joseph
  Stay the Same

Carter, Sean
　Girl's Best Friend
　Jigga My N..
Casey, Brandon
　He Can't Love You
Casey, Brian
　He Can't Love You
Castanzo, Marc
　Steal My Sunshine
Castleman, Robert *see* Kass, R. L.
Chambers, Gordon
　No More Rain in This Cloud
Chambers, Guy
　Millennium
Chapman, Beth Neilsen
　Almost Home
Chapman, Tracy
　Baby Can I Hold You
Chase, Lincoln
　Heartbreaker
Chesney, Kenny
　You Had Me from Hello
Child, Desmond
　Livin' La Vida Loca
　Shake Your Bon Bon
Chriss, Anthony
　Jamboree
Christian, Roger
　Don't Worry Baby
Christopher, James Hampton
　New Ways to Dream
　Surrender
Ciccone, Madonna Louise Veronica *see*
　Madonna
Clark, Guy
　Red River
the Clash
　Will 2K
Cochran, Wayne
　Last Kiss
Cockburn, Bruce
　Pacing the Cage
Cohen, Jeffrey
　Heartbreaker
Cohen, Leonard
　So Long Marianne
Cohen, Wayne
　Love Keep Us Together

Coleman, Cy
　Boom Boom
　What You Don't Know About Women
Coles, Dennis
　Ex-Factor
Colin, Charlie
　Meet Virginia
Collen, Phil
　Promises
Collingwood, Chris
　Troubled Times
Collins, Jim
　Hands of a Working Man
Collins, Phil
　Strangers Like Me
　You'll Be in My Heart
Collins, Tarik
　Silent Treatment
Collins, Walter
　Believe
Combs, Sean
　All Night Long
　Satisfy You
Commerford, Timothy
　Born of a Broken Man
　Guerrilla Radio
Cook, Quentin Leo
　Praise You
Cooley, Dave
　Better Days (and the Bottom Drops
　　Out)
Coomer, Ken
　Can't Stand It
　Summer Teeth
　Via Chicago
Copeland, Zane
　Anywhere
Cornell, Chris
　Can't Change Me
Cox
　He Can't Love You
Cox, Brian
　Get Gone
Cox, Tim
　Everybody's Free (to Wear Sunscreen)
Coyne, Wayne
　Race for the Prize
　Waitin' for a Superman

Crawford, Schon
  All Night Long
Crawford, Shep
  We Can't Be Friends
Cray, Robert
  All the Way
Cronin, Rich
  Girl on TV
  Summer Girls
Crosby, David
  Stand and Be Counted
Crow, Sheryl
  Anything But Down
Crowe, Greg
  Lonely and Gone
Crowell, Rodney
  Please Remember Me
Cummings, Burton
  American Woman
Cuniff, Jill
  Nervous Breakthrough
Curtis, Mike
  Choices
Daly, Eric Blair
  Hold on to Me
Damon, Delvis
  U Know What's Up
Daniels, LeShawn
  If You Had My Love
  It's Not Right But It's Okay
Danski
  We Like to Party
Darby, Ken
  This Friendly World
Davis, Diandra
  Who Dat
Davis, John
  My Ritual
Davis, Stephen
  Stand Beside Me
De La Rocha, Zack
  Born of a Broken Man
  Guerrilla Radio
Dean, Kasseem
  Girl's Best Friend
  Gotta Man
  Jigga My N..
  What Ya Want

Debarge, Eldra
  I Want It All
Debarge, R.
  I Want It All
Deere, Jason
  Little Goodbyes
DeLange, Tom
  What's My Age Again
Deleo, Dean
  Down
Delmundo, D. J.
  We Like to Party
Delong, Tom
  All the Small Things
Dennis, Charles
  Buffy the Vampire Slayer
DePaul, Gene
  I'm Past My Prime
Destri, Jimmy
  Maria
Dewese, Moe
  Wild Wild West
Diamond, Gregg
  Steal My Sunshine
Dickerson, Kenny
  If You (Lovin' Me)
DiFranco, Ani
  Angel Food
  Everest
  Jukebox
  Up Up Up Up Up Up
Diggs, Robert
  Ex-Factor
Dimant, Leo
  Re-Arranged
Drozd, Steven
  Race for the Prize
  Waitin' for a Superman
Dulaney, Michael
  What Do You Say
Dunn, Ronnie
  I Can't Get over You
Duplesis, Jerry
  My Love Is Your Love
Duritz, Adam
  Hanging Around

Durst, William
  Nookie
  Re-Arranged
Dylan, Bob
  Chimes of Freedom
  Don't Think Twice
  Fur Slippers
Earle, Steve
  Carrie Brown
  I'm Still in Love with You
Eastwood, Clint
  Why Should I Care
Ebb, Fred
  Nowadays
Edge
  Conversation on a Barstool
Edmunds, Kenneth *see* Babyface
Edmunds, Kenny *see* Babyface
Eldridge, Doug
  Why I'm Here
Ellington, Edward Kennedy "Duke"
  Something to Live For
Elliott, Melissa *see* Elliott, Missy
Elliott, Missy
  All N My Grill
  Hot Boyz
  Where My Girls At
Elliston, Shirley
  Heartbreaker
Elofsson, Joergen
  Sometimes
  You Drive Me Crazy
Emosia
  Hey Leonardo (She Likes Me for Me)
Ennis, Seamus
  I Will Remember You (Live)
Erickson, Duke
  Special
Erna, Sully
  Keep Away
Erwin, Emily
  You Were Mine
Esparza, Glenn
  Climb to Safety
Estes, Tony
  It's Not Right But It's Okay
Etheridge, Melissa
  Angels Would Fall

Evans, Dave *see* Edge
Evans, Faith
  All Night Long
Evans, Sara
  No Place That Far
Evers, J.
  Get It on Tonite
Ewing, Skip
  Wish You Were Here
  You Had Me from Hello
Falkner, Jason
  I Already Know
Fareed, Kamaal
  Vivrant Thing
Farina, Richard
  Pack up Your Sorrows
Farr, Michael
  Mas Tequila
Farrar, Charles
  Sweet Lady
Farrier, Charles
  Every Morning
Ferrell, Edward
  U Know What's Up
Ferrell, Rick
  Something Like That
Fisk, Steve
  Battle Flag
Flea
  Around the World
  Scar Tissue
Flowers, Thomas
  Why I'm Here
Fogerty, John
  Down on the Corner
Folds, Ben
  Regrets
Follese, Adrienne
  I Love You
Follese, Keith
  I Love You
  Something Like That
Foo Fighters
  Learn to Fly
Ford
  No Pigeons
Foster, Denzil
  Satisfy You

Foster, Michael
Take Me There
Foster, Radney
Anyone Else
Francis, Mary
Tonight the Heartache's on Me
Frank, David
Genie in a Bottle
The Hardest Thing
Franks, Michael
Popsicle Toes
Frazier, Charles
Falls Apart
Friedman, Kinky
Marilyn and Joe
Friedman, Richard F. *see* Friedman, Kinky
Frizell, Lefty
That's the Way Love Goes
Frusciante, John
Around the World
Scar Tissue
Full Force
All I Have to Give
Fusari, Robert
Wild Wild West
Gabutti, Massimo
Blue (Da Ba Dee)
Gadd, Paul
Mas Tequila
Gagel, Wally
My Ritual
Gaither, Todd
All Night Long
Garrett, Stephen
So Anxious
Garvin, Michael
Waiting for Tonight
Gaye, Marvin
Sexual Healing
Geiger, Mike
Hillbilly Shoes
Gibson, Dave
Lonely and Gone
Gilbert, Gillian
Blue Monday
Gill, Vince
Don't Come Crying to Me

Gist, Keir
Jamboree
Glitter, Gary
Mas Tequila
Golson, Benny
Jamboree
Goodrum, Randy
Lesson in Leavin'
Gordon, Ricky Ian
The Best for You
Finding Home
Space
We Will Always Walk Together
Gray, Macy
I've Committed Murder
Gray, Matthew
Believe
Gray, Terius *see* Juvenile
Grech, Ric
Ooh Las Vegas
Green, Marv
Amazed
Green, T.
Holla Holla
Greenberg, Kenny
Little Goodbyes
Greene, R.
Satisfy You
Grice, Greg
Ex-Factor
Griffin, Warren
I Want It All
Griffin, William
Re-Arranged
Griggs, Andy
I'll Go Crazy
You Won't Ever Be Lonely
Gripp, Parry
Buffy the Vampire Slayer
Hagar, Sammy
Mas Tequila
Hailey, Cedric
Tell Me It's Real
Will 2K
Hale, T. W.
A Night to Remember
Hall, Richard Melville *see* Moby

Hamilton, Anthony
  U Know What's Up
Hamlisch, Marvin
  Ex-Factor
Hammett, Kirk
  No Leaf Clover
Hanson, Beck
  Sexx Laws
Hardin, Tim
  Don't Make Promises
  Reason to Believe
Harper, Ben
  Burn to Shine
Harrington, Connie
  Ordinary Life
Harris, Emmylou
  Ordinary Heart
Harris, James, III
  Chante's Got a Man
  Give It to You
Hart, Beth
  L.A. Song
Hart, Emerson
  You Wanted More
Hartman, Mark
  Calling My Baby Back
Haseltine, Dan
  Unforgetful You
Hayes, Darron
  The Animal Song
  I Knew I Loved You
Hedges, Ray
  C'est La Vie
Henderson, Christopher
  Happily Ever After
Hendricks, Matt
  With You
Henry, Michael
  I Love You Came Too Late
Hersh, Kristin
  Cathedral Heat
  Echo
Hetfield, James
  No Leaf Clover
Hewson, Paul *see* Bono
Hicks, Kevin
  Get Gone

Higgins, Brian
  Believe
Hill, Dan
  I Do (Cherish You)
  She's in Love
Hill, Edward
  Whatever You Say
Hill, Lauryn
  All That I Can Say
  Everything Is Everything
  Ex-Factor
Holland, Bryan
  Why Don't You Get a Job
Hollister, Dave
  My Favorite Girl
Holmes, Rory
  Staying Power
Holyfield, Wayland
  Meanwhile
Hook, Peter
  Blue Monday
Hopkins, Beth
  Moment of Weakness
Hopkins, Mark
  What's My Age Again
Hoppus, Mark
  All the Small Things
Hornsby, Bruce
  Changes
Hotchkiss, Rob
  Meet Virginia
Houston, Marques
  Stay the Night
Howell
  No Pigeons
Hubbard, Gregg
  Drive Me Wild
Hubbard, Leonard
  Silent Treatment
Hudson, Saul *see* Slash
Hugo, Chad
  Caught out There
  Got Your Money
Hummon, Marcus
  Ready or Not
  Ready to Run
Hunt, Dana
  Write This Down

Hunt, Timothy
All Things Considered
Hurley, Michael
Tea Song
Hyler, Tammy
I Love You
Hynde, Chrissie
Dragway 42
Ian, Janis
At Seventeen
Irby, Jerry
Drivin' Nails in My Coffin
Isaac, Gerald
Your Child
Isaac, Tony
Stay the Night
Ivanisevich, Ric
Why I'm Here
Ivins, Michael
Race for the Prize
Waitin' for a Superman
Jackson, Alan
Gone Crazy
Little Man
Jackson, George
Chante's Got a Man
Jagger, Mick
Party Doll
James, Thomas
Wrong Again
Jean, Wyclef
My Love Is Your Love
Jeffers, Eve
Gotta Man
What Ya Want
Jenkins, Stephan
New Girl
Jennings, Will
Please Remember Me
Jerkins, Fred
If You Had My Love
It's Not Right But It's Okay
Jerkins, Rodney
If You Had My Love
It's Not Right But It's Okay
John, Elton
Elaborate Lives
Not Me

A Step Too Far
Written in the Stars
Johnson, Carolyn
Single White Female
Johnson, Errol
Sitting Home
Johnson, Michael
Empty Hearts
Johnston, Tonya
4, 5, 6
Who Dat
Jones, Daniel
The Animal Song
I Knew I Loved You
Jones, Daron
Anywhere
Jones, Jerome
Stay the Night
Jones, Russell
Got Your Money
Jones, Tom
They Were You
Jones, William
You Won't Ever Be Lonely
Jones, Willie
I'm Not Ready
Jordan, E.
I Want It All
Jordan, Jeremy
A Girl Named Happiness (Never Been Kissed)
Jordan, Montell
Get It on Tonite
Jordan, Steven A.
My Favorite Girl
Joseph, Jerry
Climb to Safety
Juvenile
Back That Thang Up
Kahne, David
Every Morning
Falls Apart
Someday
Kale, M. J.
American Woman
Kander, John
Nowadays

Lyricists & Composers Index

Karges, Matthew
  Falls Apart
Karlin, Kenneth
  Heartbreak Hotel
  It's All About You (Not About Me)
Karroll, Peter
  Moment of Weakness
Kass, R. L.
  Forget About It
Keidis, Anthony
  Around the World
  Scar Tissue
Keith, Michael
  Anywhere
Kelis
  Caught out There
Kelly, Robert
  Did You Ever Think
  808
  Fortunate
  If I Could Turn Back Time
  Satisfy You
  When a Woman's Fed Up
Kennedy, Gordon
  Lost in You
Kenny, Charles
  Laughing at Life
Kenny, Nick
  Laughing at Life
Kidd, Jonathan
  Shakin' All Over
Kilcher, Jewel
  Down So Long
Kinchen, Marc
  My Favorite Girl
King, Jay
  Satisfy You
King, Wesley
  This Is Your Time
Kipner, Steve
  Genie in a Bottle
  The Hardest Thing
Kipper
  A Thousand Years
Kirkpatrick, Wayne
  Lost in You
Knight, Baker
  Lonesome Town

Knight, Jack
  Sitting Home
Knight, Jordan
  Give It to You
Knobloch, Fred
  Meanwhile
Knowles, Beyonce
  Bills Bills Bills
  Bug a Boo
Korduletsch, Jurgen
  Get It on Tonite
Korn
  Falling Away from Me
Kottle, Tameka
  No Pigeons
  No Scrubs
Koutrakous, Lina
  Calling My Baby Back
Kowalczyk, Ed
  The Dolphin's Cry
Kramer, David
  Cavala Kings
Kreuger, David
  Sometimes
  You Drive Me Crazy
LaChuisa, Robert John
  Way Back to Paradise
Lamar, Holly
  Breathe
Landau, Tina
  The Best for You
  Finding Home
  Space
  We Will Always Walk Together
Lane, Ronnie
  Ooh La La
Lange, Robert John
  Come on Over
  Man I Feel Like a Woman
  Promises
  That Don't Impress Me Much
  You've Got a Way
Lashley, Nick
  No Pressure Over Cappucino
Lauderdale, Jim
  Another Sinner's Prayer
  I Already Loved You
  What Do You Say to That

Lavery, Dan
  You Wanted More
Lawler, Mike
  Drive Me Wild
Lawrence, B. K.
  Bring It All to Me
Lawrence, Ron
  All Night Long
Leander, Mike
  Mas Tequila
Leiber, Jerry
  One Bad Stud
Leigh, Carolyn
  Boom Boom
Lennox, Annie
  17 Again
Leo, Josh
  Wrong Night
Levert, Gerald
  Taking Everything
Levy, Hal
  Blue Jean Bop
Lewis, Aaron
  Mudshovel
Lewis, Al
  Tears on My Pillow
Lewis, Keni
  If You Love Me
Lewis, L.
  Bring It All to Me
Lewis, Terry
  Chante's Got a Man
  Give It to You
Light, Sara
  Home to You
Lighty, Clifton
  U Know What's Up
Lighty, Darren
  U Know What's Up
Lil Wayne
  Back That Thang Up
  Bling Bling
Lim, Jinsoo
  I Try
Lincoln, Abbey
  Caged Bird
Lindsay, Chris
  Amazed

Lippa, Andrew
  My New Philosophy
Little, Joe
  I'm Not Ready
Littrell, Brian
  Larger Than Life
Lobina, Maurizio
  Blue (Da Ba Dee)
Logan, Harold
  Where Were You on Our Wedding
  Day
London, Mark
  To Sir with Love
Lopez, Jennifer
  If You Had My Love
Lorenzo, Irving
  Holla Holla
Love, Larry
  Woke up This Morning
Lovelace, Kelly
  He Didn't Have to Be
Lowell, Charlie
  Unforgetful You
Luckett, LeToya
  Bills Bills Bills
  Bug a Boo
Lumpkins, Heavynn
  It's All About You (Not About Me)
Lundin, Kristian
  Larger Than Life
  That's the Way It Is
Luongo, Chuck
  A Girl Named Happiness (Never Been
  Kissed)
Lynch, Edele
  C'est La Vie
Lynch, Keavy
  C'est La Vie
Lynott, Phil
  The Boys Are Back in Town
Macrae, Johnny
  Tonight the Heartache's on Me
Madonna
  Beautiful Stranger
Magnusson, Per
  You Drive Me Crazy
Maher, Brent
  Lesson in Leavin'

Lyricists & Composers Index

Malkmus, Stephen
  Ann Don't Cry
  Major Leagues
  Spit on a Stranger
Mandile, Stephen
  For a Little While
Mann, Aimee
  Momentum
  Save Me
  Wise Up
Mann, Barry
  Out in the Streets
Mannie Fresh
  Back That Thang Up
  Bling Bling
Manson, Shirley
  Special
Marchand, Pierre
  Angel
Marker, Steve
  Special
Marley, Bob
  Turn Your Lights down Low
Marsden, Pauline
  Pack up Your Sorrows
Martin, Anthony
  No Place That Far
  Whatever You Say
Martin, Max
  I Want It That Way
  Larger Than Life
  That's the Way It Is
  You Drive Me Crazy
Martin, Tony
  I'll Think of a Reason Later
Marx, Richard
  If You Leave Me
Mason, Steve
  Unforgetful You
Matthews, Dave
  Crush
  Love of My Life
Mavers, Lee Anthony
  There She Goes
Maxwell, Lamont
  Anywhere
Mayfield, Curtis
  Did You Ever Think

Mayo, Aimee
  Amazed
McBride, Jim
  I Can't Get over You
McCorvey, Bill
  Lonely and Gone
McDonald, Michael
  Empty Hearts
McElroy, Thom
  Satisfy You
McGrath, Mark
  Every Morning
  Falls Apart
McIntyre, Joe
  Stay the Same
McIntyre, Natalie
  I Try
McKagen, Duff
  Sweet Child of Mine
McKnight, Brian
  Back at One
  Hold Me
McLachlan, Sarah
  Angel
  I Will Remember You (Live)
McLennan, Stuart
  Believe
Meeks, Travis
  Enemy
Mellin, Robert
  Stranger on the Shore
Mercedes, Tony
  Who Dat
Mercer, Johnny
  I'm Past My Prime
Mercury, Freddie
  Crazy Little Thing Called Love
Merenda, Dave
  I Will Remember You (Live)
Merrill, Bob
  Music That Makes Me Dance
Michael, George
  One More Try
Miller, Mark A.
  Drive Me Wild
Miller, Zyshonne see Silkk the Shocker

Mills, Mike
  At My Most Beautiful
  The Great Beyond
Mitchell, Joni
  The Magdelene Laundries
Mize, Ben
  Hanging Around
Mobley, Wendell
  How Forever Feels
Moby
  Porcelain
Monahan, Patrick
  Meet Virginia
Money, J. T.
  Who Dat
Montgomery, Melba
  What Do You Say to That
Moore, Chante
  Chante's Got a Man
Moore, Debbie
  Wish You Were Here
Moore, Sergio
  Get It on Tonite
Morello, Tom
  Born of a Broken Man
  Guerrilla Radio
Morissette, Alanis
  No Pressure Over Cappucino
Morris, Steven
  Blue Monday
Morrison, Bob
  Tonight the Heartache's on Me
Morrison, Van
  When the Leaves Come Falling Down
Mosley, Tim
  All N My Grill
  Hot Boyz
Muhammed, Balewa
  U Know What's Up
Mullins, Tony
  How Forever Feels
Mullis, Woody
  Hillbilly Shoes
Mushok, Mike
  Mudshovel
Mystikal
  It Ain't My Fault

Nash, George
  Spend My Life with You
NdegeOcello, Me Shell
  Satisfy
Nelsen, Reid
  Don't Come Crying to Me
Nelson, Fred Jr.
  Why I'm Here
Nelson, Madeline
  Take Me There
Nelson, Marc
  15 Minutes
Nelson, Prince Rogers see Prince
Newman, Randy
  Feels Like Home
  I Miss You
  I'm Dead (But I Don't Know It)
  My Country
  The Time of Your Life
  When She Loved Me
Newton, Johari
  Everything Is Everything
Nichol, Joseph
  Every Morning
  Falls Apart
Nichols, Tim
  I'll Think of a Reason Later
Nilsson, Harry
  One
Nixon, Mojo
  Rock and Roll Hall of Lame
Noriega, Jorge
  Shake Your Bon Bon
  She's All I Ever Had
Nowels, Rick
  You Get What You Give
O'Brien, Dillon
  How Do I Deal
Ochs, Phil
  I Ain't Marchin' Anymore
O'Connor, Sinead
  C'est La Vie
Odmark, Matt
  Unforgetful You
Oliver, Tony
  Stay the Night

Lyricists & Composers Index

Olivier, Jean Claude
 Did You Ever Think
 Hold Me
Orbit, William
 Beautiful Stranger
Orteca, Rainy
 Baby Love
Orton, Beth
 Central Reservation
 Pass in Time
 Stars All Seem to Weep
 Stolen Car
Osborn, Kristyn
 Little Goodbyes
Osborne, Joan
 Baby Love
Otto, John
 Nookie
 Re-Arranged
Overbig, Geoff
 One More Try
Page, Stephen
 Get in Line
Paisley, Brad
 He Didn't Have to Be
Palmer, Brian
 Get It on Tonite
Parker, Quinnes
 Anywhere
Parker, Trey
 Blame Canada
 Eyes of a Child
Parsons, Chris
 High Fashion Queen
Parsons, Gram
 High Fashion Queen
 One Hundred Years from Now
 Ooh Las Vegas
 Return of the Grievous Angel
Partridge, Andy
 The Last Balloon
 Your Dictionary
Paschal, Joey
 Staying Power
Patrick, Richard
 Take a Picture
Patton, A.
 All N My Grill

Patton, John
 Where Were You on Our Wedding
  Day
Peiken, Shelly
 Almost Doesn't Count
 What a Girl Wants
Pena, Federico
 Satisfy
Pence, Jeff
 Hey Leonardo (She Likes Me for Me)
Penna, Erik
 Baby Love
Perkins, Carl
 Movie Magg
Peters, Gretchen
 The Secret of Life
Peterson, Garry
 American Woman
Peterson, Taliep
 Cavala Kings
Petruzelli, Jack
 Baby Love
Petty, Tom
 Free Girl Now
 Room at the Top
Phillips, Eddie
 Making Time
Phillips, Isaac
 It's Not Right But It's Okay
Photoglo, Jim
 You Give Me Love
Pickett, Ken
 Making Time
Pitney, Gene
 I'm Gonna Be Strong
Pollard, Robert
 Hold on Hope
Popoff, Alan
 My Own Worst Enemy
Popoff, Jeremy
 My Own Worst Enemy
Posey, Demonte
 Spend My Life with You
Powell, Jesse
 You
Powell, Timothy
 Believe

Prado, Perez
  Mambo No. 5 (A Little Bit of..)
Prestwood, Hugh
  Ghost in This House
Price, Kelly
  Satisfy You
Price, Lloyd
  Where Were You on Our Wedding
    Day
Prince
  Battle Flag
  Greatest Romance Ever Sold
  1999
Prine, John
  Back Street Affair
  In Spite of Ourselves
Rambeaux, Will
  Never Been Kissed
Rambeaux, William
  Hold on to Me
Randone
  Blue (Da Ba Dee)
Ray, Angelo
  24/7
Raymond, James
  Stand and Be Counted
Read, Sean
  Stolen Car
Reed, Bertram
  All Night Long
Reed, Natina
  808
Renald, James
  Love Song
Renn, Volt
  Love All over Again
Reznor, Trent
  The Day the World Went Away
  We're in This Together
Rhodes, Kimmie
  Ordinary Heart
Rice, Tim
  Elaborate Lives
  Not Me
  A Step Too Far
  Written in the Stars
Riley, Teddy
  Take Me There

Ritchie, Robert
  Bawitdaba
  Cowboy
Ritz, David
  Sexual Healing
Rivers, Samuel
  Nookie
  Re-Arranged
Robbins, Kent
  Write This Down
Robbins, Marty
  Don't Worry
Roberson, Antoinette
  If You (Lovin' Me)
  Taking Everything
  What's It Gonna Be
Robertson, Elliott
  Get in Line
Robertson, Latavia
  Bug a Boo
Robinson, Bobby
  Will 2K
Robinson, D.
  I Want It All
Roboff, Annie
  Almost Home
Roche, Guy
  Almost Doesn't Count
  What a Girl Wants
Rodgers, Evan
  God Must Have Spent a Little More
    Time on You
Roland, Carl
  You
Roland, Ed
  Heavy
Rooney, Corey
  Bring It All to Me
  I Need to Know
  If You Had My Love
Rosa, Robi
  Livin' La Vida Loca
  Shake Your Bon Bon
  She's All I Ever Had
Rose, Axl
  Oh My God
  Sweet Child of Mine

Lyricists & Composers Index

Rossdale, Gavin
  The Chemicals Between Us
Rowland, Kelendria
  Bills Bills Bills
  Bug a Boo
Roy, Phil
  How Do I Deal
Ruby, L
  Bring It All to Me
Rucker, Sharon
  Marilyn and Joe
Russaw, Todd
  All Night Long
Russell, J.
  We Can't Be Friends
Russell, Tom
  Love Abides
Russo, Jeff
  You Wanted More
Ruzumna, Jeremy
  I Try
  I've Committed Murder
Ryan, Terry
  I'm Already Taken
Rzeznik, Johnny
  Black Balloon
Safka, Melanie
  Lay Down (Candles in the Rain)
Sager, Carole Bayer
  Why Should I Care
Salter, Sam
  15 Minutes
Santana, Carlos
  Love of My Life
Savage, Tamara
  Heartbreak Hotel
  Take Me There
  When I Close My Eyes
Scaggs, William
  We're All Alone
Scalzo, Tony
  Out of My Head
Scandrick, Marvin
  Anywhere
Schack, Carsten
  Heartbreak Hotel
  It's All About You (Not About Me)

Schellenbach, Kathy
  Nervous Breakthrough
Schlesinger, Adam
  Troubled Times
Schmidt, Harvey
  They Were You
Schrody, Erik *see* Schrody, Everlast
Schrody, Everlast
  Put Your Lights On
  What It's Like
Schwartz, Stephen
  Tear Me Down
  When You Believe (Prince of Egypt)
Scott, Bon
  Highway to Hell
Scott, David
  24/7
Scott, Jill
  You Got Me
Seats, Eric
  Where My Girls At
Secada, Jon
  She's All I Ever Had
Seidel, Martie
  Ready or Not
  Ready to Run
  You Were Mine
Selby, Mark
  In 2 Deep
Serletic, Matt
  Back 2 Good
Sewell, Marvin
  Right Here, Right Now
Sexsmith, Ron
  Beautiful View
  Right About Now
Sexton, Martin
  Love Keep Us Together
Shafer, Eric
  Bawitdaba
  Cowboy
Shafer, Sanger
  That's the Way Love Goes
Shaiman, Marc
  Blame Canada
  Eyes of a Child
Shakur, Tupac
  Changes

Shanks, John
  Angels Would Fall
Shapiro, Tom
  No Place That Far
Sharp, Bree
  David Duchovny
Shaw, Tommy
  Number One
Shelby, W.
  Bring It All to Me
Shellenberger, Allen
  My Own Worst Enemy
Shepherd, Kenny Wayne
  In 2 Deep
Sheppard, Rodney
  Every Morning
  Falls Apart
Sherlock, Stephen
  Buffy the Vampire Slayer
Sheyne, Pam
  Genie in a Bottle
Shur, Itaal
  Smooth
Sicotte, Antoine
  Love Song
Siffre, Claudius
  My Name Is
Silkk the Shocker
  It Ain't My Fault
Sims, Matt
  Better Days (and the Bottom Drops
    Out)
Sims, Tommy
  Lost in You
Sixx, Nikki
  Too Fast for Love
Skinner, Jolyon
  Love All over Again
Slash
  Sweet Child of Mine
Sloan, Elliot
  Hey Leonardo (She Likes Me for Me)
Slocum, Matt
  Kiss Me
Smith, Anthony
  24/7
Smith, Arlen
  Home to You

Smith, Chad
  Around the World
  Scar Tissue
Smith, Michael W.
  This Is Your Time
Smith, Rashad
  What's It Gonna Be
Smith, Shawn
  Battle Flag
Smith, Shaye
  Single White Female
Smith, Will
  Wild Wild West
  Will 2K
Sondheim, Stephen
  Delighted I'm Sure
  Exhibit A
  I Remember That
Spencer, K.
  Bring It All to Me
Spirit
  Woke up This Morning
Springsteen, Bruce
  Across the Border
  The Promise
Stafford, Jimmy
  Meet Virginia
Staley, Layne
  Get Born Again
Stampfel, Peter
  Tea Song
Stapp, Scott
  Higher
  One
Steele, Jeffrey
  Big Deal
  Unbelievable
Stegall, Keith
  I Do (Cherish You)
  She's in Love
Steinman, Jim
  No Matter What
Stewart, Christopher
  4, 5, 6
  Who Dat
Stewart, Dave
  17 Again

Lyricists & Composers Index

Stewart, Rapture
  Where My Girls At
Stewart, Sylvester
  Thank You (Falletten Me Be Myself
    Again)
Sting
  King of Pain
  A Thousand Years
Stinson, Harry
  You Give Me Love
Stipe, Michael
  At My Most Beautiful
  The Great Beyond
Stirratt, John
  Can't Stand It
  Summer Teeth
  Via Chicago
Stoller, Mike
  One Bad Stud
Stone, Angie
  No More Rain in This Cloud
Storch, Scott
  Silent Treatment
  You Got Me
Stradlin, Izzy
  Sweet Child of Mine
Strayhorn, Billy
  Something to Live For
Stuckey, Nat
  Pop a Top
Sturken, Carl
  God Must Have Spent a Little More
    Time on You
Styne, Jule
  Music That Makes Me Dance
Sugar Ray
  Falls Apart
  Someday
Sumner, Bernard
  Blue Monday
Sumner, Gordon see Sting
Swann, Gregg
  I've Committed Murder
Swanston, Nigel
  Everybody's Free (to Wear Sunscreen)
Sweat, Keith
  I'm Not Ready

Sweet, Matthew
  Faith in You
Sylvers, N.
  Bring It All to Me
Tab
  15 Minutes
Tate, Danny
  In 2 Deep
Taylor, Bobby
  Hillbilly Shoes
Taylor, Mark
  Bailamos
Taylor, Troy
  Sweet Lady
Tedeschi, Susan
  Looking for Answers
Tellez, Pablo
  Every Morning
Temple, Philip
  Waiting for Tonight
Thabigo, Nkhereanye
  Who Dat
Thicke, Robin
  Give It to You
Thiele, Bob Jr.
  How Do I Deal
Thomas, Damon
  Never Gonna Let You Go
  These Are the Times
Thomas, Joe
  Faded Pictures
Thomas, Rob
  Back 2 Good
  Smooth
Thompkins, Jeffrey Jermaine
  4, 5, 6
Thompson, Ahmir
  Silent Treatment
  You Got Me
Thompson, Joshua
  Faded Pictures
Thompson, Linda
  Why Should I Care
Thompson, Richard
  Crawl Back (under My Stone)
  Hard on Me
Thrasher, Neil
  What Do You Say

Tifrere, Mashonda
  Girl's Best Friend
  Gotta Man
Todd, Cornell
  Laughing at Life
Todd, Joshua
  For the Movies
  Lit Up
Torch, Steve
  Believe
Traditional
  Whiskey in the Jar
Trask, Stephen
  Angry Inch
Travis, John
  Bawitdaba
  Cowboy
Travis, Merle
  Smoke Smoke Smoke That Cigarette
Tremonti, Mark
  Higher
  One
Trimble, Viv
  Nervous Breakthrough
Trombly, James
  Bawitdaba
  Cowboy
Trotter, Tarik
  You Got Me
Trudell, John
  Dizzy Duck
Turman, Nicolia
  15 Minutes
Turner
  All the Way
Turner, Zack
  I'll Go Crazy
Turpin, Sonnyboy
  My Favorite Girl
Turpin, William see Turpin, Sonnyboy
Twain, Shania
  Come on Over
  Man I Feel Like a Woman
  That Don't Impress Me Much
  You've Got a Way
Tweedy, Jeff
  Can't Stand It

  Summer Teeth
  Via Chicago
Tyler, Michael see Mystikal
Ulrich, Lars
  No Leaf Clover
Underwood, Galen
  All Night Long
Underwood, Scott
  Meet Virginia
Van Horsen, L.
  Bring It All to Me
Van Zandt, Townes
  To Live Is to Fly
Vandiver, Jerry
  For a Little While
Vassar, Phil
  For a Little While
Vaughn, Sharon
  Powerful Thing
Vickrey, Dan
  Hanging Around
Vig, Butch
  Special
Vincent, Gene
  Blue Jean Bop
Wainwright, Loudon
  Tonya's Twirls
  You're Older Than You've Ever Been
Waits, Tom
  Big in Japan
  Come on up to the House
  Hold On
  House Where Nobody Lives
  What's He Building
Walden, Narada Michael
  Heartbreaker
Walker, Butch
  Freak of the Week
Walker, Jeffrey
  Satisfy You
Wariner, Steve
  I'm Already Taken
  Two Teardrops
Warner, Brian
  Rock Is Dead
Warren, Diane
  Blue Eyes Blue
  Can't Take That Away (Mariah's

Theme)
Faith of the Heart
I Could Not Ask for More
I Don't Want to Miss a Thing
I Learned from the Best
I Will Get There
I'll Still Love You More
Love Is All That Matters
Loving You Is All I Know
Music of My Heart
My First Night with You
Nothing Can Keep Me from You
Watkins, Tionne
  Tionne's Song
  Unpretty
Watters, Sam
  I Wanna Love You Forever
Weatherly, Jim
  No More Rain in This Cloud
Webber, Andrew Lloyd
  New Ways to Dream
  No Matter What
  Surrender
Weil, Cynthia
  Out in the Streets
  Wrong Again
Weiland, Scott
  Down
White, Eric Foster
  I Love You Came Too Late
White, Jeordie
  Rock Is Dead
Whitehead, Kenneth
  Sitting Home
Wilder, David
  I Try
Wildhorn, Frank
  Freedom's Child
Wilk, Brad
  Born of a Broken Man
  Guerrilla Radio
Williams, Bobby
  No More Rain in This Cloud
Williams, Dar
  If I Wrote You
Williams, David
  Hands of a Working Man

Williams, Pharrell
  Caught out There
  Got Your Money
Williams, Robbie
  Angels
  Millennium
Williams, Tex
  Smoke Smoke Smoke That Cigarette
Wilson, A.
  Get It on Tonite
Wilson, Brian
  Don't Worry Baby
Wilson, Cassandra
  Right Here, Right Now
Wilson, William
  I'll Go Crazy
Winchester, Jesse
  That's What Makes You Strong
Winwood, Stevie
  Can't Find My Way Home
Wonder, Stevie
  Wild Wild West
Wood, Ron
  Ooh La La
Woodard, Case
  Happily Ever After
Woods, Corey
  Ex-Factor
Wright, Erica
  Southern Gul
Wysocki, Jim
  Mudshovel
Yarborough, Camille
  Praise You
Yates, Billy
  Choices
Young, Angus
  Highway to Hell
Young, Brad
  Girl on TV
  Summer Girls
Young, Neil
  Looking Forward
  Out of Control
  Slowpoke
Zarate, Abel
  Every Morning
Zimmerman, Robert Allen see Dylan,
  Bob

Zippel, David
   What You Don't Know About Women

Zippy
   Mambo No. 5 (A Little Bit of..)

Important Performances Index

Songs are listed under the works in which they were introduced or given significant renditions. The index is organized into major sections by performance medium: Album, Movie, Musical, Performer, Revue, Television Show.

Album

Affirmation
  I Knew I Loved You
All the Pain Money Can Buy
  Out of My Head
All the Way..A Decade of Song
  That's the Way It Is
Always Never the Same
  Meanwhile
  What Do You Say to That
  Write This Down
The American
  Love Keep Us Together
American Pie
  New Girl
  You Wanted More
Americana
  Why Don't You Get a Job
Amplified
  Vivrant Thing
Apple Venus Volume 1
  The Last Balloon
  Your Dictionary
Astralounge
  All Star
Astro Lounge
  Then the Morning Comes

Austin Powers: The Spy Who Shagged
  Me
  American Woman
  Beautiful Stranger
Avenue B
  Shakin' All Over
..Baby One More Time
  Sometimes
Back at One
  Back at One
  Hold Me
Back on Top
  When the Leaves Come Falling Down
Bad Love
  I Miss You
  I'm Dead (But I Don't Know It)
  My Country
The Battle of Los Angeles
  Born of a Broken Man
  Guerrilla Radio
Beach House on the Moon
  Pacing the Cage
Before These Crowded Streets
  Crush
Believe
  Believe

121

The Best Man
  Turn Your Lights down Low
Best Of
  Changes
Betty Buckley's Broadway
  New Ways to Dream
  Surrender
Big Daddy
  Sweet Child of Mine
Bitter
  Satisfy
Black Diamond
  No More Rain in This Cloud
Blaque
  Bring It All to Me
  808
Bleecker Street: Greenwich Village in the '60s
  I Ain't Marchin' Anymore
  Pack up Your Sorrows
  Reason to Believe
  So Long Marianne
Blue Indian
  Dizzy Duck
Blue Streak
  Girl's Best Friend
'Bout It
  You
Brand New Day
  A Thousand Years
Brave New World
  Number One
Breakdown
  Angels Would Fall
Breathe
  Breathe
  The Secret of Life
Buckcherry
  For the Movies
  Lit Up
Buffy the Vampire Slayer
  Buffy the Vampire Slayer
A Bug's Life
  The Time of Your Life
Burn to Shine
  Burn to Shine
Butterfly
  Heartbreaker

B*Witched
  C'est La Vie
Californication
  Around the World
  Scar Tissue
Can You Still Feel
  I Already Know
Candy Ass
  Blue Monday
Central Reservation
  Central Reservation
  Pass in Time
  Stars All Seem to Weep
  Stolen Car
Chad Brock
  Ordinary Life
The Championship Season
  They Were You
Charlotte Church
  Just Wave Hello
A Cheap and Evil Girl
  David Duchovny
Cheating at Solitaire
  Don't Think Twice
Chocolate Mood
  15 Minutes
Chopper City in the Ghetto
  Bling Bling
Christina Aguilera
  Genie in a Bottle
  What a Girl Wants
Cold Dog Soup
  Red River
Cold Hard Truth
  Choices
Come on Over
  Come on Over
  Man I Feel Like a Woman
  That Don't Impress Me Much
Cruel Moon
  I'm Gonna Be Strong
Da Real World
  All N My Grill
  Hot Boyz
Daddy & Them
  In Spite of Ourselves
A Day in the Life
  Spend My Life with You

The Days of Our Nights
  Sweet Child of Mine
Days of the New
  Enemy
Deconstruction
  Lay Down (Candles in the Rain)
Detroit Rock City
  The Boys Are Back in Town
  Highway to Hell
  Nothing Can Keep Me from You
Devil Without a Cause
  Bawitdaba
  Cowboy
The Distance to Here
  The Dolphin's Cry
Dizzy Up the Girl
  Black Balloon
D'Lectrified
  When I Said I Do
Do the Collapse
  Hold on Hope
Dosage
  Heavy
Drive Me Crazy
  Unforgetful You
  You Drive Me Crazy
Drive Me Wild
  Drive Me Wild
Drive You Home Again
  Don't Make Promises
Dysfunction
  Mudshovel
Echo
  Free Girl Now
  Room at the Top
EDTV
  Thank You (Falletten Me Be Myself
    Again)
The Ego Has Landed
  Millennium
18 Tracks
  The Promise
E.L.E. Extinction Level Event
  What's It Gonna Be
Electric Honey
  Nervous Breakthrough
Elton John's Aida
  Elaborate Lives

Not Me
  A Step Too Far
  Written in the Stars
Emotion
  I Love You
  Whatever You Say
  Wrong Again
End of Days
  Oh My God
Enema of the State
  All the Small Things
  What's My Age Again
Enter the Dru
  These Are the Times
Euphoria
  Promises
Euphoria Morning
  Can't Change Me
Europop
  Blue (Da Ba Dee)
Every Day Is a New Day
  Love Is All That Matters
Everywhere We Go
  How Forever Feels
  You Had Me from Hello
Fairy Tales
  One More Try
Fan Mail
  No Scrubs
  Unpretty
A Far Cry from Dead
  To Live Is to Fly
February Sun
  Why I'm Here
Finally
  Take Me There
Fly
  Ready or Not
  Tonight the Heartache's on Me
  You Were Mine
For the Love of the Game
  Baby Love
For the Record
  That's the Way Love Goes
Forever
  Satisfy You
Forget About It
  Empty Hearts

Forget About It
  Ghost in This House
4
  Down
400 Degreez
  Back That Thang Up
14:59
  Every Morning
  Falls Apart
  Someday
The Fragile
  The Day the World Went Away
  We're in This Together
From Broken Hearts to Blue Skies
  Laughing at Life
  Losing Hand
  Something to Live For
Garage, Inc.
  Whiskey in the Jar
Gentleman of Leisure
  That's What Makes You Strong
Get It on Tonite
  Get It on Tonite
Get Skintight
  Too Fast for Love
Ghetto Hymns
  My Favorite Girl
The Globe Sessions
  Anything But Down
Go
  Steal My Sunshine
Godsmack
  Keep Away
Happy Texas
  Ordinary Heart
Heart and Soul: New Songs from Ally
  McBeal, Featuring Vonda Shepherd
  To Sir with Love
Hedwig and the Angry Inch
  Angry Inch
  Tear Me Down
Hey Album
  Freak of the Week
Hi Lo Country
  Drivin' Nails in My Coffin
  Smoke Smoke Smoke That Cigarette

High Mileage
  Gone Crazy
  Little Man
Home to You
  Hold on to Me
  Home to You
The Hot Rock
  Size of Our Love
  Start Together
Hours
  Thursday's Child
How to Operate with a Blown Mind
  Battle Flag
Human Clay
  Higher
  One
I Bificus
  Moment of Weakness
I Don't Want to Miss a Thing
  I Don't Want to Miss a Thing
I Feel Like Singing Today
  Another Sinner's Prayer
I Still Know What You Did Last Summer
  How Do I Deal
I Wanna Be Kate
  Running up That Hill
I Want It All
  I Want It All
Ideal
  Get Gone
If I Left the Zoo
  Unforgetful You
I'm Alright
  Lesson in Leavin'
  Powerful Thing
  Stand Beside Me
In Reverse
  Faith in You
In Spite of Ourselves
  Back Street Affair
In the Life of Chris Gaines
  Lost in You
Introducing Michael Fredo
  Love All over Again
Issues
  Falling Away from Me
It's Real
  Tell Me It's Real

J.E. Heartbreak
  He Can't Love You
Jonatha Brooke Live
  Is This All
Jordan Knight
  Give It to You
Just Won't Burn
  Looking for Answers
The Kaleidoscope
  Caught out There
Kat and the Kings
  Cavala Kings
Keep the Faith
  All Night Long
  Never Gonna Let You Go
The Key
  Don't Come Crying to Me
Kima, Keisha and Pam
  Sitting Home
King of the Hill
  Down on the Corner
  Get in Line
Last Chance for a Thousand Years
  Crazy Little Thing Called Love
LeAnn Rimes
  Big Deal
  Don't Worry
Let There Be..Eve-Ruff Ryders' First
  Lady
  What Ya Want
LFO
  Girl on TV
  Summer Girls
Life
  Fortunate
Life's Aquarium
  If You Love Me
Liquid Skin
  Revolutionary Kind
A Little Bit of Mambo
  Mambo No. 5 (A Little Bit of..)
Live from Australia
  Back 2 Good
Live in Concert
  Space Oddity
Live On
  In 2 Deep

Lonely Grill
  Amazed
Looking Forward
  Looking Forward
  Out of Control
  Slowpoke
  Stand and Be Counted
Love and Consequences
  Taking Everything
Love in the Real World
  Never Been Kissed
A Love Like Ours
  If You Leave Me
  Music That Makes Me Dance
Made Man
  It Ain't My Fault
Magnolia
  Momentum
  One
  Save Me
  Wise Up
Main Stage Live: Falcon Ridge Folk
  Festival
  If I Wrote You
Make the Music 2000
  Southern Gul
The Man from God Knows Where
  Love Abides
Man on the Moon
  The Great Beyond
  This Friendly World
Marc Anthony
  I Need to Know
Mary
  All That I Can Say
  Your Child
The Matrix
  Rock Is Dead
Maybe You've Been Brainwashed Too
  You Get What You Give
Memory of the Future
  Rain Falls down in Amsterdam
Message in a Bottle
  I Could Not Ask for More
Midnight Vultures
  Sexx Laws
Millennium
  All I Have to Give

125

Angels
I Want It That Way
Larger Than Life
Mirror Ball
Angel
I Will Remember You (Live)
The MisEducation of Lauryn Hill
Everything Is Everything
Ex-Factor
Mobile Estates
Better Days (and the Bottom Drops
Out)
Mock Tudor
Crawl Back (under My Stone)
Hard on Me
Mod Squad
Can't Find My Way Home
The Mountain
Carrie Brown
I'm Still in Love with You
MTV Unplugged
King of Pain
No Pressure Over Cappucino
Mule Variations
Big in Japan
Come on up to the House
Hold On
House Where Nobody Lives
What's He Building
Music of the Heart
Music of My Heart
My Favorite Broadway: The Leading
Ladies Live at Carnegie Hall
Nowadays
My Love Is Your Love
Heartbreak Hotel
I Learned from the Best
It's Not Right But It's Okay
My Love Is Your Love
Mya
My First Night with You
'N Sync
God Must Have Spent a Little More
Time on You
Never Been Kissed
A Girl Named Happiness (Never Been
Kissed)

Never Say Never
Almost Doesn't Count
Nigga Please
Got Your Money
A Night to Remember
A Night to Remember
19 Naughty Nine: Nature's Fury
Jamboree
98 and Rising
The Hardest Thing
No Boundaries
Last Kiss
No Exit
Maria
Out in the Streets
No Place That Far
No Place That Far
Nothing Safe: The Best of the Box
Get Born Again
Nottinghill
I Do (Cherish You)
No Matter What
You've Got a Way
NRBQ
Pain
On How Life Is
I Try
I've Committed Murder
On the 6
If You Had My Love
Waiting for Tonight
100% Ginuwine
So Anxious
One Part Lullaby
My Ritual
One Wish
We Can't Be Friends
Onward Through It All
I Already Loved You
The Other Sister
The Animal Song
Loving You Is All I Know
Parade
All the Wasted Time
It's Not over Yet
The Party Album
We Like to Party

Party Doll and Other Favorites
  Almost Home
  Party Doll
Patch Adams
  Faith of the Heart
Peace
  17 Again
Pearls in the Snow: The Songs of Kinky
  Friedman
  Marilyn and Joe
A Perfect Stranger
  Conversation on a Barstool
Permanently
  Back at One
Personal Conversation
  Faded Pictures
  Happily Ever After
Piece of Paradise
  Love Song
Pimpin' on Wax
  Who Dat
A Place in the Sun
  For a Little While
  My Own Worst Enemy
  Please Remember Me
  Something Like That
Play
  Porcelain
Prince of Egypt
  I Will Get There
  When You Believe (Prince of Egypt)
R.
  Did You Ever Think
  If I Could Turn Back Time
  When a Woman's Fed Up
Rainbow
  Can't Take That Away (Mariah's
    Theme)
Rave un2 the Joy Fantastic
  Greatest Romance Ever Sold
The Real Sock Ray Blue
  Rock and Roll Hall of Lame
Red Voodoo
  Mas Tequila
Return of the Grievous Angel: A Tribute
  to Gram Parsons
  High Fashion Queen
  One Hundred Years from Now

Ooh Las Vegas
Return of the Grievous Angel
Sleepless Nights
Ricky Martin
  Livin' La Vida Loca
  Shake Your Bon Bon
  She's All I Ever Had
Room 112
  Anywhere
The Roots Come Alive
  Silent Treatment
Ruff Ryder's First Lady
  Gotta Man
Run Devil Run
  Blue Jean Bop
  Lonesome Town
  Movie Magg
Runaway Bride
  Blue Eyes Blue
  Ready to Run
  Where Were You on Our Wedding
    Day
Rushmore
  Making Time
  Ooh La La
Rx
  You Don't Miss Your Water
Ryde or Die Compilation
  Jigga My N..
S&M
  No Leaf Clover
Science of Things
  The Chemicals Between Us
Screaming for My Supper
  L.A. Song
The Sebadoh
  Weird
Secret of Giving
  Wrong Night
702
  Where My Girls At
Shake, Rattle & Roll
  Fur Slippers
  One Bad Stud
  Tears on My Pillow
Shanice
  When I Close My Eyes

She Talks to Rainbows
  Don't Worry Baby
She's All That
  Kiss Me
Significant Other
  Nookie
  Re-Arranged
Single White Female
  Single White Female
Sixpence None the Richer
  There She Goes
The Sixties
  Chimes of Freedom
Skin Deep
  4, 5, 6
Sky Motel
  Cathedral Heat
  Echo
The Slim Shady Lp
  My Name Is
Smartie Mine
  Joe van Gogh
  Krautmeyer
So Good Together
  We're All Alone
  What Do You Say
Social Studies
  Tonya's Twirls
  You're Older Than You've Ever Been
The Soft Bulletin
  Race for the Prize
  Waitin' for a Superman
Some Things I Know
  I'll Think of a Reason Later
Something for Everybody
  Everybody's Free (to Wear Sunscreen)
Something in the Air
  With You
Somewhere Between Heaven and Earth
  Better Than I've Ever Been
Songs in the Key of G
  Stranger on the Shore
The Sopranos
  Woke up This Morning
South Park: Bigger, Longer & Uncut
  Blame Canada
  Eyes of a Child

Spirit
  Down So Long
Stay the Same
  I Love You Came Too Late
  Stay the Night
  Stay the Same
Staying Power
  Staying Power
Steam
  Hands of a Working Man
Still in the Game
  I'm Not Ready
Street Cinema
  No Pigeons
Summer Teeth
  Can't Stand It
  Summer Teeth
  Via Chicago
Supernatural
  Love of My Life
  Put Your Lights On
  Smooth
Sweet Kisses
  I Wanna Love You Forever
Take Your Shoes Off
  All the Way
Tal Bachman
  She's So High
Tarzan
  Strangers Like Me
  You'll Be in My Heart
Tattoos and Scars
  Hillbilly Shoes
  Lonely and Gone
Teaching Mrs. Tingle
  At Seventeen
Tears of Stone
  The Magdelene Laundries
Terror Twilight
  Ann Don't Cry
  Major Leagues
  Spit on a Stranger
There Is Nothing Left to Lose
  Learn to Fly
Things Fall Apart
  You Got Me
This Desert Life
  Hanging Around

This Is Your Time
  This Is Your Time
This Moment Is Mine
  Chante's Got a Man
Thoughts
  Tionne's Song
Tiempas
  Dia a Dia (Every Day)
Tiempos
  Vida (Life)
Tight Rope
  I Can't Get over You
Til the Medicine Takes
  Climb to Safety
Timeless (The Classics) Vol. 2
  Sexual Healing
Title of Record
  Take a Picture
To Venus and Back
  Bliss
  1000 Oceans
Tonight
  If You (Lovin' Me)
Too Much Fun
  Tea Song
Toy Story II
  When She Loved Me
Tracie
  It's All About You (Not About Me)
Train
  Meet Virginia
Travelling Miles
  Right Here, Right Now
Trio II
  Feels Like Home
True Crime
  Why Should I Care
Twentieth Century
  God Must Have Spent a Little More
    Time on You
24/7
  24/7
Two Teardrops
  I'm Already Taken
  Two Teardrops
Tyrese
  Sweet Lady

Unauthorized Biography of Reinhold
  Masoner
  Regrets
Unbelievable
  Unbelievable
Unconditional Love
  Did You Ever Know
Under the Influence
  Pop a Top
Unsuspecting Hearts
  I'm Past My Prime
  What You Don't Know About Women
Untamed
  All Things Considered
Up
  At My Most Beautiful
Up Up Up Up Up Up
  Angel Food
  Everest
  Jukebox
  Up Up Up Up Up Up
Utopia Parkway
  Troubled Times
Venni, Vetti, Vecci
  Holla Holla
Version 2.0
  Special
Viva El Amor
  Dragway 42
Walking off the Buzz
  Hey Leonardo (She Likes Me for Me)
Walls Come Down
  Anyone Else
Western Wall: The Tucson Sessions
  Across the Border
  For a Dancer
When I Look in Your Eyes
  Popsicle Toes
  When I Look in Your Eyes
When the Pawn..
  Fast as You Can
  I Know
  On the Bound
  Paper Bag
Where I Wanna Be
  U Know What's Up
Where We Belong
  Baby Can I Hold You

Where Your Road Leads
  I'll Still Love You More
Whereabouts
  Beautiful View
  Right About Now
Whitey Ford Sings the Blues
  What It's Like
Who Needs Pictures
  He Didn't Have to Be
The Whole Shebang
  Little Goodbyes
Wholly Earth
  Caged Bird
Wild Wild West
  Bailamos
  Wild Wild West
Willennium
  Will 2K
Wish You Were Here
  She's in Love
  Wish You Were Here
The World Is Not Enough
  The World Is Not Enough
The Writing's on the Wall
  Bills Bills Bills
  Bug a Boo
You Won't Ever Be Lonely
  I'll Go Crazy
  You Won't Ever Be Lonely
You've Come a Long Way Baby
  Praise You

Movie

American Pie
  New Girl
  You Wanted More
Austin Powers: The Spy Who Shagged
  Me
  American Woman
  Beautiful Stranger
The Best Man
  Turn Your Lights down Low
Big Daddy
  Sweet Child of Mine
Blue Streak
  Girl's Best Friend

A Bug's Life
  The Time of Your Life
Daddy & Them
  In Spite of Ourselves
Detroit Rock City
  The Boys Are Back in Town
  Highway to Hell
  Nothing Can Keep Me from You
Double Platinum
  Love Is All That Matters
Drive Me Crazy
  Unforgetful You
  You Drive Me Crazy
EDTV
  Thank You (Falletten Me Be Myself
    Again)
End of Days
  Oh My God
For the Love of the Game
  Baby Love
Go
  Steal My Sunshine
Happy Texas
  Ordinary Heart
Hi Lo Country
  Drivin' Nails in My Coffin
  Smoke Smoke Smoke That Cigarette
I Still Know What You Did Last Summer
  How Do I Deal
Life
  Fortunate
Magnolia
  Momentum
  One
  Save Me
  Wise Up
Man on the Moon
  The Great Beyond
  This Friendly World
The Matrix
  Rock Is Dead
Message in a Bottle
  I Could Not Ask for More
Mod Squad
  Can't Find My Way Home
Music of the Heart
  Music of My Heart

Mystery Men
   All Star
Never Been Kissed
   A Girl Named Happiness (Never Been
      Kissed)
Nottinghill
   I Do (Cherish You)
   No Matter What
   You've Got a Way
The Other Sister
   The Animal Song
   Loving You Is All I Know
Patch Adams
   Faith of the Heart
Prince of Egypt
   I Will Get There
   When You Believe (Prince of Egypt)
Romeo & Juliet
   Everybody's Free (to Wear Sunscreen)
Runaway Bride
   Blue Eyes Blue
   Ready to Run
   Where Were You on Our Wedding
      Day
Rush Hour
   Faded Pictures
Rushmore
   Making Time
   Ooh La La
She's All That
   Kiss Me
South Park: Bigger, Longer & Uncut
   Blame Canada
   Eyes of a Child
Tarzan
   Strangers Like Me
   You'll Be in My Heart
Teaching Mrs. Tingle
   At Seventeen
Toy Story II
   When She Loved Me
True Crime
   Why Should I Care
Wild Wild West
   Bailamos
   Wild Wild West
The World Is Not Enough
   The World Is Not Enough

Musical

The Civil War
   Freedom's Child
Dreams True
   The Best for You
   Finding Home
   Space
   We Will Always Walk Together
Hedwig and the Angry Inch
   Angry Inch
   Tear Me Down
Kat and the Kings
   Cavala Kings
Little Me
   Boom Boom
Parade
   It's Not over Yet
Saturday Night
   Delighted I'm Sure
   Exhibit A
   I Remember That
You're a Good Man Charley Brown
   My New Philosophy

Operetta

Marie Christine
   Way Back to Paradise

Performer

Aguilera, Christina
   Genie in a Bottle
   What a Girl Wants
Alabama
   God Must Have Spent a Little More
      Time on You
Alice in Chains
   Get Born Again
Amos, Tori
   Bliss
   1000 Oceans
Anderson, Eric
   Rain Falls down in Amsterdam
Anthony, Marc
   I Need to Know
Apple, Fiona
   Fast as You Can

I Know
On the Bound
Paper Bag
A3
Woke up This Morning
Austin, Sherrie
Never Been Kissed
B. G.
Bling Bling
Baby
Bling Bling
Bachman, Tal
She's So High
Backstreet Boys
All I Have to Give
I Want It That Way
Larger Than Life
Badu, Erykah
Southern Gul
You Got Me
The Baltimores
Running up That Hill
Barenaked Ladies
Get in Line
Beck
Drivin' Nails in My Coffin
Sexx Laws
Bega, Lou
Mambo No. 5 (A Little Bit of..)
Ben Folds Five
Regrets
Ben Harper and the Innocent Criminals
Burn to Shine
Benet, Eric
Spend My Life with You
Bergman, Mary Kay
Blame Canada
Bern, Dan
Joe van Gogh
Krautmeyer
Song for the Children
Bif Naked
Moment of Weakness
Big Boi
All N My Grill
Black, Clint
When I Said I Do

Black 47
I Ain't Marchin' Anymore
Blacksheep
Take Me There
Blades, Ruben
Dia a Dia (Every Day)
Vida (Life)
Blaque
Bring It All to Me
808
Blessid Union of Souls
Hey Leonardo (She Likes Me for Me)
Blige, Mary J.
All That I Can Say
Your Child
Blink 182
All the Small Things
What's My Age Again
Blinky Blink
Take Me There
Blondie
Maria
Out in the Streets
Bolton, Michael
Sexual Healing
Bowie, David
Thursday's Child
Boyz II Men
I Will Get There
Not Me
Boyzone
Baby Can I Hold You
No Matter What
Brandy
Almost Doesn't Count
Brock, Chad
Ordinary Life
Brooke, Jonatha
Is This All
Brooks & Dunn
I Can't Get over You
Brooks, Meredith
Lay Down (Candles in the Rain)
Brown, Sally
My New Philosophy
Bryant, Kobe
Hold Me

Bryson, Peabo
  Did You Ever Know
Buckcherry
  For the Movies
  Lit Up
Buckley, Betty
  New Ways to Dream
  Surrender
Buffett, Jimmy
  Pacing the Cage
Bullens, Cindy
  Better Than I've Ever Been
Bush
  The Chemicals Between Us
B*Witched
  C'est La Vie
Cale, John
  So Long Marianne
Callier, Terry
  Pass in Time
Carey, Mariah
  Can't Take That Away (Mariah's
    Theme)
  Heartbreaker
  When You Believe (Prince of Egypt)
Carmello, Carolee
  All the Wasted Time
  It's Not over Yet
Carpenter, Mary Chapin
  Almost Home
  Party Doll
Carrey, Jim
  This Friendly World
Carver, Brent
  All the Wasted Time
  It's Not over Yet
Cast
  Cavala Kings
Cast of Civil War
  Freedom's Child
Chenoweth, Kristen
  My New Philosophy
Cher
  Believe
Chesney, Kenny
  How Forever Feels
  You Had Me from Hello

Chesnutt, Mark
  I Don't Want to Miss a Thing
The Chieftains
  The Magdelene Laundries
Church, Charlotte
  Just Wave Hello
Citizen King
  Better Days (and the Bottom Drops
    Out)
Clapton, Eric
  Blue Eyes Blue
Clark, Guy
  Red River
Collective Soul
  Heavy
Collins, Phil
  Strangers Like Me
  You'll Be in My Heart
Cook, Barbara
  They Were You
Cornell, Chris
  Can't Change Me
Costello, Elvis
  Sleepless Nights
Counting Crows
  Hanging Around
Cowboy Junkies
  Ooh Las Vegas
Cox, Deborah
  We Can't Be Friends
Cray, Robert
  All the Way
Creation
  Making Time
Creed
  Higher
  One
Crosby, David
  Return of the Grievous Angel
Crosby, Stills, Nash & Young
  Looking Forward
  Out of Control
  Slowpoke
  Stand and Be Counted
Crow, Sheryl
  Anything But Down
  Sweet Child of Mine

Daddy, Puff
  All Night Long
Dave Matthews Band
  Crush
Davis, Alana
  Can't Find My Way Home
Days of the New
  Enemy
Dee, Kool Moe
  Wild Wild West
Def Leppard
  Promises
the Del McCoury Band
  Carrie Brown
DeMent, Iris
  I'm Still in Love with You
Dement, Iris
  In Spite of Ourselves
  Pack up Your Sorrows
Destiny's Child
  Bills Bills Bills
  Bug a Boo
Diamond Rio
  Unbelievable
Diffie, Joe
  A Night to Remember
DiFranco, Ani
  Angel Food
  Everest
  Jukebox
  Up Up Up Up Up Up
Dion, Celine
  That's the Way It Is
Divine
  One More Try
Dixie Chicks
  Ready or Not
  Ready to Run
  Tonight the Heartache's on Me
  You Were Mine
the Donnas
  Too Fast for Love
Dylan, Bob
  Chimes of Freedom
Earle, Steve
  Carrie Brown
  High Fashion Queen
  I'm Still in Love with You

Edmunds, Kevon
  24/7
Eiffel 65
  Blue (Da Ba Dee)
Elliott, Missy 'Misdemeanor'
  All N My Grill
  Hot Boyz
Eminem
  My Name Is
Ensemble of Dreams True
  Space
Estefan, Gloria
  Music of My Heart
Ethridge, Melissa
  Angels Would Fall
Eurythmics
  17 Again
Evans, Faith
  All Night Long
  Never Gonna Let You Go
Evans, Sara
  No Place That Far
Eve
  Gotta Man
  Hot Boyz
  What Ya Want
Everclear
  The Boys Are Back in Town
Everlast
  Put Your Lights On
  What It's Like
The Faces
  Ooh La La
Faithfull, Marianne
  Conversation on a Barstool
Falkner, Jason
  I Already Know
Fastball
  Out of My Head
Fatboy Slim
  Praise You
Filter
  Take a Picture
Fitchen, Samantha
  I Remember That
the Flaming Lips
  Race for the Prize
  Waitin' for a Superman

The Folk Implosion
  My Ritual
Foo Fighters
  Learn to Fly
Fountains of Wayne
  Troubled Times
Fredo, Michael
  Love All over Again
Friedman, Kinky
  Marilyn and Joe
Gaines, Chris
  Lost in You
Garbage
  Special
  The World Is Not Enough
Gill, Vince
  Don't Come Crying to Me
  If You Leave Me
Ginuwine
  So Anxious
Godsmack
  Keep Away
Gomez
  Revolutionary Kind
Goo Goo Dolls
  Black Balloon
Gray, Macy
  I Try
  I've Committed Murder
Green, Al
  To Sir with Love
Griggs, Andy
  I'll Go Crazy
  You Won't Ever Be Lonely
Guided by Voices
  Hold on Hope
Guns N' Roses
  Oh My God
Hadley, Heather
  A Step Too Far
Hagar, Sammy
  Mas Tequila
Haggard, Merle
  That's the Way Love Goes
Harris, Emmylou
  Across the Border
  Feels Like Home

For a Dancer
  Ordinary Heart
Hart, Beth
  L.A. Song
Hawkins, Brad
  One Bad Stud
Headley, Heather
  Elaborate Lives
Herndon, Ty
  Hands of a Working Man
Hersh, Kristin
  Cathedral Heat
  Echo
Hewitt, Jennifer Love
  How Do I Deal
Hill, Dru
  These Are the Times
  Wild Wild West
Hill, Faith
  Breathe
  The Secret of Life
  You Give Me Love
Hill, Lauryn
  Everything Is Everything
  Ex-Factor
  Turn Your Lights down Low
Hillman, Chris
  High Fashion Queen
Hollister, Dave
  My Favorite Girl
Holy Modal Rounders
  Tea Song
Houston, Whitney
  Heartbreak Hotel
  I Learned from the Best
  It's Not Right But It's Okay
  My Love Is Your Love
  When You Believe (Prince of Egypt)
Ideal
  Get Gone
Iglesias, Enrique
  Bailamos
Ja Rule
  Holla Holla
Jackson, Alan
  Gone Crazy
  Little Man
  Pop a Top

Jackson, Janet
  What's It Gonna Be
Jagged Edge
  He Can't Love You
Jars of Clay
  Unforgetful You
Jay Z
  Girl's Best Friend
  Heartbreaker
  Jigga My N..
Jenkins, Arnel
  We Will Always Walk Together
Jewel
  Down So Long
  That's the Way Love Goes
Joe
  Faded Pictures
Joel, Billy
  Where Were You on Our Wedding
    Day
John, Elton
  A Step Too Far
  Written in the Stars
JoJo
  Tears on My Pillow
  Tell Me It's Real
Jones, Donell
  U Know What's Up
Jones, George
  Choices
Jones, Kacey
  Marilyn and Joe
Jordan, Jeremy
  A Girl Named Happiness (Never Been
    Kissed)
Jordan, Montell
  Get It on Tonite
Juvenile
  Back That Thang Up
  Bling Bling
K-Ci
  Tears on My Pillow
  Tell Me It's Real
  Will 2K
Kandi
  4, 5, 6
Karvelas, Charles
  Exhibit A

Kelis
  Caught out There
  Got Your Money
Kelly, R.
  Did You Ever Think
  If I Could Turn Back Time
  Satisfy You
  When a Woman's Fed Up
Kenny G
  Stranger on the Shore
Kenny Wayne Shepherd Band
  In 2 Deep
Kid Rock
  Bawitdaba
  Cowboy
King, B. B.
  Fur Slippers
Kiss
  Nothing Can Keep Me from You
Knight, Jordan
  Give It to You
Korn
  Falling Away from Me
Koutrakos, Lina
  Calling My Baby Back
Krall, Diana
  Popsicle Toes
  When I Look in Your Eyes
  Why Should I Care
Krauss, Alison
  Empty Hearts
  Forget About It
  Ghost in This House
Kravitz, Lenny
  American Woman
Kuhn, Judy
  The Best for You
Lauderdale, Jim
  Another Sinner's Prayer
  I Already Loved You
Len
  Steal My Sunshine
Levert, Gerard
  Taking Everything
LFO
  Girl on TV
  Summer Girls

Lil Wayne
  Back That Thang Up
  Bling Bling
Lil 'Z
  Anywhere
Limp Bizkit
  Nookie
  Re-Arranged
Lincoln, Abbey
  Caged Bird
Lit
  My Own Worst Enemy
Live
  The Dolphin's Cry
Lo Fidelity All Stars
  Battle Flag
Lonestar
  Amazed
Lopez, Jennifer
  If You Had My Love
  Waiting for Tonight
Loveless, Patty
  Back Street Affair
Luhrman, Baz
  Everybody's Free (to Wear Sunscreen)
Luna
  Sweet Child of Mine
Luscious Jackson
  Nervous Breakthrough
Madonna
  Beautiful Stranger
Mann, Aimee
  Momentum
  One
  Save Me
  Wise Up
Mannie Fresh
  Back That Thang Up
  Bling Bling
Manson, Marilyn
  Highway to Hell
  Rock Is Dead
Marley, Bob
  Turn Your Lights down Low
Martin, Ricky
  Livin' La Vida Loca
  Shake Your Bon Bon
  She's All I Ever Had

Marvelous 3
  Freak of the Week
Matchbox 20
  Back 2 Good
Matthews, Dave
  Love of My Life
the Mavericks
  Down on the Corner
Maxwell
  Fortunate
McBride, Martina
  I Love You
  Whatever You Say
  Wrong Again
McCain, Edwin
  I Could Not Ask for More
McCann, Lila
  With You
McCarthy, Jeff
  The Best for You
  Space
McCartney, Paul
  Blue Jean Bop
  Lonesome Town
  Movie Magg
McCorkle, Susannah
  Laughing at Life
  Losing Hand
  Something to Live For
McDonald, Audra
  Way Back to Paradise
McDonald, Michael
  Eyes of a Child
McEntire, Reba
  We're All Alone
  What Do You Say
  Wrong Night
McGraw, Tim
  For a Little While
  Please Remember Me
  Something Like That
McIntyre, Joey
  I Love You Came Too Late
  Stay the Night
  Stay the Same
McKnight, Brian
  Back at One
  Hold Me

McLachlan, Sarah
  Angel
  I Will Remember You (Live)
  When She Loved Me
McLaskey, Jessica
  Finding Home
McLean, Tara
  At Seventeen
Merchant, Natalie
  Space Oddity
Messina, Jo Dee
  Lesson in Leavin'
  Powerful Thing
  Stand Beside Me
Metallica
  No Leaf Clover
  Whiskey in the Jar
Miller, Buddy
  I'm Gonna Be Strong
Mint Condition
  If You Love Me
Mr. Woods
  No Pigeons
Mitchell, John Cameron
  Angry Inch
  Tear Me Down
Mitchell, Joni
  The Magdelene Laundries
Moby
  Porcelain
Money, J. T.
  4, 5, 6
  Who Dat
Montgomery Gentry
  Hillbilly Shoes
  Lonely and Gone
Montgomery, John Michael
  Hold on to Me
  Home to You
Moore, Chante
  Chante's Got a Man
Morissette, Alanis
  King of Pain
  No Pressure Over Cappucino
Morrison, Van
  When the Leaves Come Falling Down

Mya
  My First Night with You
  Take Me There
Mystikal
  It Ain't My Fault
'N Sync
  God Must Have Spent a Little More
    Time on You
  Music of My Heart
Nas
  Hot Boyz
Naughty By Nature
  Jamboree
NdegeOcello, Me Shell
  Satisfy
Nelson, Marc
  15 Minutes
Nelson, Willie
  Drivin' Nails in My Coffin
Nerf Herder
  Buffy the Vampire Slayer
Ness, Mike
  Don't Think Twice
Neuwirth, Bebe
  Nowadays
New Radicals
  You Get What You Give
Newman, Randy
  I Miss You
  I'm Dead (But I Don't Know It)
  My Country
  The Time of Your Life
Nicole
  All N My Grill
Nine Inch Nails
  The Day the World Went Away
  We're in This Together
98 Degrees
  The Hardest Thing
  I Do (Cherish You)
Nixon, Mojo
  Rock and Roll Hall of Lame
Nokio
  What Ya Want
NRBQ
  Pain
the Offspring
  Why Don't You Get a Job

Ol' Dirty Bastard
  Got Your Money
Oleander
  Why I'm Here
112
  Anywhere
Orgy
  Blue Monday
Orton, Beth
  Central Reservation
  Pass in Time
  Stars All Seem to Weep
  Stolen Car
Osborne, Joan
  Baby Love
  Chimes of Freedom
Paisley, Brad
  He Didn't Have to Be
Parton, Dolly
  Feels Like Home
Pavement
  Ann Don't Cry
  Major Leagues
  Spit on a Stranger
Pearl Jam
  Last Kiss
Pegasus Players
  Delighted I'm Sure
Petty, Tom
  Free Girl Now
  Room at the Top
Pop, Iggy
  Shakin' All Over
Powell, Jesse
  You
the Pretenders
  Dragway 42
Pretenders
  Loving You Is All I Know
Prince
  Greatest Romance Ever Sold
  1999
Prine, John
  Back Street Affair
  In Spite of Ourselves
Puff Daddy
  Satisfy You

Q-Tip
  Hot Boyz
  Vivrant Thing
Queen Latifah
  Lay Down (Candles in the Rain)
Rage Against the Machine
  Born of a Broken Man
  Guerrilla Radio
Rahzel
  Southern Gul
Raye, Collin
  Anyone Else
Red Hot Chili Peppers
  Around the World
  Scar Tissue
R.E.M.
  At My Most Beautiful
  The Great Beyond
  This Friendly World
Rhymes, Busta
  What's It Gonna Be
Rimes, LeAnn
  Big Deal
  Don't Worry
  Written in the Stars
Ripley, Alice
  I'm Past My Prime
  What You Don't Know About Women
Ronstadt, Linda
  Across the Border
  Feels Like Home
  For a Dancer
The Roots
  Silent Treatment
  You Got Me
Ross, Diana
  Love Is All That Matters
Russell, Tom
  Love Abides
Santana
  Love of My Life
  Put Your Lights On
  Smooth
Savage Garden
  The Animal Song
  I Knew I Loved You
Sawyer Brown
  Drive Me Wild

Scott, Sherie
  A Step Too Far
Sebadoh
  Weird
702
  Where My Girls At
Sexsmith, Ron
  Beautiful View
  Reason to Believe
  Right About Now
Sexton, Martin
  Love Keep Us Together
Shanice
  When I Close My Eyes
Sharp, Bree
  David Duchovny
Shedaisy
  Little Goodbyes
Shepherd, Vonda
  To Sir with Love
Short, Martin
  Boom Boom
Silk
  If You (Lovin' Me)
Silkk the Shocker
  It Ain't My Fault
Simpson, Jessica
  I Wanna Love You Forever
Sixpence None the Richer
  Kiss Me
  There She Goes
Skinner, Emily
  I'm Past My Prime
  What You Don't Know About Women
Sky
  Love Song
Sleater-Kinney
  Size of Our Love
  Start Together
Smash Mouth
  All Star
  Then the Morning Comes
Smith, Michael W.
  This Is Your Time
Smith, Will
  Wild Wild West
  Will 2K

Smither, Chris
  Don't Make Promises
Sole
  4, 5, 6
Spears, Britney
  Sometimes
  You Drive Me Crazy
Spector, Ronnie
  Don't Worry Baby
Spencer, Tracie
  It's All About You (Not About Me)
Sporty Thievz
  No Pigeons
Springsteen, Bruce
  The Promise
Staind
  Mudshovel
Stanley, Ralph
  Another Sinner's Prayer
Stanton, Harry Dean
  You Don't Miss Your Water
Stewart, Rod
  Faith of the Heart
Sting
  A Thousand Years
Stone, Angie
  No More Rain in This Cloud
Stone Temple Pilots
  Down
Strait, George
  Meanwhile
  What Do You Say to That
  Write This Down
Streisand, Barbra
  If You Leave Me
  Music That Makes Me Dance
Stuart, Marty
  Smoke Smoke Smoke That Cigarette
Styx
  Number One
Sugar Ray
  Every Morning
  Falls Apart
  Someday
Sweat, Keith
  I'm Not Ready
Sweet, Matthew
  Faith in You

Tamia
  Spend My Life with You
Tedeschi, Susan
  Looking for Answers
Third Eye Blind
  New Girl
Thomas, Rob
  Smooth
Thompson, Richard
  Crawl Back (under My Stone)
  Hard on Me
TLC
  No Scrubs
  Unpretty
Tone
  Hold Me
Tonic
  You Wanted More
Total
  Sitting Home
Train
  Meet Virginia
Trudell, John
  Dizzy Duck
Turk
  Bling Bling
Twain, Shania
  Come on Over
  Man I Feel Like a Woman
  That Don't Impress Me Much
  You've Got a Way
2Pac
  Changes
Tyrese
  Sweet Lady
Van Zandt, Townes
  To Live Is to Fly
Vega, Suzanne
  So Long Marianne
Vegaboys
  We Like to Party
Wainwright, Loudon
  Pack up Your Sorrows
  Tonya's Twirls
  You're Older Than You've Ever Been
Waits, Tom
  Big in Japan
  Come on up to the House

Hold On
House Where Nobody Lives
What's He Building
Wariner, Steve
  I'm Already Taken
  Two Teardrops
Warren G.
  I Want It All
Watkins, Tionne
  Tionne's Song
White, Barry
  Staying Power
  Thank You (Falletten Me Be Myself Again)
Widespread Panic
  Climb to Safety
Wilco
  Can't Stand It
  One Hundred Years from Now
  Summer Teeth
  Via Chicago
Williams, Dar
  If I Wrote You
Williams, Lucinda
  Return of the Grievous Angel
Williams, Robbie
  Angels
  Millennium
Wills, Mark
  Back at One
  She's in Love
  Wish You Were Here
Wilson, Cassandra
  Right Here, Right Now
Winchester, Jesse
  That's What Makes You Strong
Womack, Lee Ann
  I'll Think of a Reason Later
Woodard, Case
  Faded Pictures
  Happily Ever After
Wright, Chely
  Single White Female
XTC
  The Last Balloon
  Your Dictionary
Yankee Grey
  All Things Considered

Yearwood, Trisha
  I'll Still Love You More
Yoakam, Dwight
  Crazy Little Thing Called Love
Young, Neil
  Across the Border
Zhane
  Jamboree
Ziemba, Karen
  Nowadays

Television Show

Ally McBeal
  To Sir with Love
Buffy the Vampire Slayer
  Buffy the Vampire Slayer

King of the Hill
  Down on the Corner
  Get in Line
Mad About You
  You Give Me Love
Nightline
  You're Older Than You've Ever Been
Shake, Rattle & Roll
  Fur Slippers
  One Bad Stud
  Tears on My Pillow
The Sixties
  Chimes of Freedom
The Sopranos
  Woke up This Morning

Awards Index

A list of songs nominated for Academy Awards by the Academy of Motion Picture Arts and Sciences and Grammy Awards from the National Academy of Recording Arts and Sciences. Asterisks indicate the winners; multiple listings indicate multiple nominations.

1999

Academy Award
  Blame Canada
  Music of My Heart
  Save Me
  When She Loved Me
  You'll Be in My Heart*
Grammy Award
  All That I Can Say
  Amazed
  Angels Would Fall
  Beautiful Stranger*
  Believe
  Bills Bills Bills
  Choices
  Come on Over*
  Heartbreak Hotel

I Want It That Way
It's Not Right But It's Okay
Livin' La Vida Loca
Music of My Heart
No Scrubs
No Scrubs*
The Promise
Ready to Run
Room at the Top
Scar Tissue*
Smooth*
Special
The Time of Your Life
Two Teardrops
Unpretty
When You Believe (Prince of Egypt)
You'll Be in My Heart
You've Got a Way

List of Publishers

A directory of publishers of the songs included in *Popular Music,* 1999. Publishers that are members of the American Society of Composers, Authors, and Publishers or whose catalogs are available under ASCAP license are indicated by the designation (ASCAP). Publishers that have granted performing rights to Broadcast Music, Inc., are designated by the notation (BMI). Publishers whose catalogs are represented by The Society of Composers, Authors and Music Publishers of Canada, are indicated by the designation (SOCAN). Publishers whose catalogs are represented by SESAC, Inc., are indicated by the designation (SESAC).

The addresses were gleaned from a variety of sources, including ASCAP, BMI, SOCAN, SESAC, and *Billboard* magazine. As in any volatile industry, many of the addresses may become outdated quickly. In the interim between the book's completion and its subsequent publication, some publishers may have been consolidated into others or changed hands. This is a fact of life long endured by the music business and its constituents. The data collected here, and throughout the book, are as accurate as such circumstances allow.

A

Acuff Rose Music (BMI)
  65 Music Square West
  Nashville, Tennessee 37203

Adria K Music (ASCAP)
  see Warner-Chappell Music

Al Andersongs (BMI)
  PO Box 120904
  Nashville, Tennessee 37212

J. Albert & Sons Music (ASCAP)
  c/o Freddy Bienstock Ent.
  1619 Broadway, 11th Fl.
  New York, New York 10019

Alley Music (BMI)
  1619 Broadway, 11th Fl.
  New York, New York 10019

Almo/Irving
  1358 N. LaBrea
  Los Angeles, California 90028

Almo/Irving Music (BMI)
  1358 N La Brea
  Los Angeles, California 90028

Almo Music Corp. (BMI)
  360 N. La Cienega
  Los Angeles, California 90048

145

List of Publishers

American Academy of Music, Inc. (ASCAP)
1776 Broadway
New York, New York 10019

Deric Angelettie Music (BMI)
see EMI Music Publishing

Anne-Rachel Music Corp. (ASCAP)
c/o Chappell & Co., Inc.
810 7th Ave.
New York, New York 10019

Annotation Music (ASCAP)
see Warner-Chappell Music

Anthony C. Music (ASCAP)
see Warner-Chappell Music

Anwa Music (ASCAP)
see Rondor Music Inc.

Appletree Music (BMI)
see Warner-Chappell Music

Aspen Fair Music (ASCAP)
c/o CBS
51 W. 52nd St., Ste. 2080
New York, New York 10019

Audacity Music (ASCAP)
see Chrysalis Music Group

Audible Sun (BMI)
1775 Broadway, 7th Fl.
New York, New York 10019

Ausar Music (BMI)
see EMI Music Publishing

Awkward Paws Music (ASCAP)
see EMI Music Publishing

B
B. Black Music (ASCAP)
see EMI Music Publishing

B-Rok Music (ASCAP)
see Zomba Music

Baby Little Music (ASCAP)
see Chrysalis Music Group

Baby Mae Music (BMI)
c/o Hamstein
PO Box 163870
Austin, Texas 78716

Baby Spike Music (ASCAP)
see Gifted Source Music

Babyboy's Little Music (SESAC)
see Chrysalis Music Group

Bachman & Sons Music (BMI)
see EMI Music Publishing

Balewa Music (ASCAP)
see Warner-Chappell Music

Barricade Music Inc. (ASCAP)
see Almo Music Corp.

Basically Zappo Music (ASCAP)
see Warner-Chappell Music

Bayjun Beat (BMI)
see MCA Music

Bayou Bay Music (BMI)
see Reynsong Music

Be Music
Address Unavailable

Beechwood Music (BMI)
see EMI Music Publishing

Beeswing Music (BMI)
c/o Gary Stamler
2029 Century Park, E., Ste. 1500
Los Angeles, California 90067

Beginner Music (ASCAP)
PO Box 50418
Nashville, Tennessee 37205

Maria Belle (BMI)
see Warner-Chappell Music

Belton Uncle Music (BMI)
see Acuff Rose Music

Beyonce Music (ASCAP)
see EMI Music Publishing

146

Bidnis Inc Music (BMI)
see EMI Music Publishing

Bienstock Publishing Co. (ASCAP)
see Alley Music

Big Bizkit Music (ASCAP)
see Warner-Chappell Music

Big on Blue Music (BMI)
see Warner-Chappell Music

Big Meanie Music (ASCAP)
see EMI Music Publishing

Big P Music (BMI)
1651 South Lubdill, No. 102178
Baton Rouge, Louisiana 70806

Big Prod Music (ASCAP)
see EMI Music Publishing

Big Red Tractor Music (ASCAP)
see Warner-Chappell Music

BKY Music (ASCAP)
see Trans Continental Music

Black Bull Music (BMI)
Attn: Stevland Morris
4616 Magnolia Blvd.
Burbank, California 91505

Black Fountain (ASCAP)
see BMG Music

Blackened Music (BMI)
c/o Prager & Fenton
12424 Wilshire Blvd., Ste. 1000
Los Angeles, California 90025

Blackhawk Music Co. (BMI)
1420 Marron Circle, N.E.
Albuquerque, New Mexico 87112

Blackmore Ave. Music (ASCAP)
see EMI Music Publishing

Ruben Blades Music (ASCAP)
3720 Canterbury Way
Boca Raton, Florida 33434

Blazalicious Music (ASCAP)
see Warner-Chappell Music

Bliss WG Music (ASCAP)
Address Unavailable

Blondie Rockwell Music (ASCAP)
see Warner-Chappell Music

Blood Heavy (BMI)
see Dinger & Ollie Music

Blue Khakis Music (SESAC)
see Put It Down Music

Blue Quill Music (ASCAP)
see MCA, Inc.

Blue Sky Rider Songs (BMI)
c/o Prager and Fenton
6363 Sunset Blvd., Ste. 706
Los Angeles, California 90028

Bluewater (BMI)
see Polygram Music Publishing Inc.

BMG Music (ASCAP)
1540 Broadway
New York, New York 10036

BMG Scandinavia Music
Address Unavailable

BNC (ASCAP)
see Almo/Irving Music

Bobby Robinson Music (BMI)
see Zomba Music

Boondocks Music (ASCAP)
c/o Calhoun Ent.
Box 515
White Bluffs, Tennessee 37187

Brandon & Brody Music (BMI)
see Warner-Chappell Music

Brentwood Music (BMI)
1 Maryland Farms, Ste. 200
Brentwood, Tennessee 37021

Bridge Building Music (BMI)
see Brentwood Music

List of Publishers

Bro N' Sis Music (BMI)
see Keith Sykes Music

Brother 4 Brothers (ASCAP)
see Warner-Chappell Music

Bucks Music
Address Unavailable

Bud Dog Music (ASCAP)
see We Make Music

Buddah Music Inc. (ASCAP)
see United Artists Music Co., Inc.

Bug Music (BMI)
Bug Music Group
6777 Hollywood Blvd., 9th Fl.
Hollywood, California 90028

Burning Field Music (BMI)
see Bug Music

Edgar Rice Burroughs Music (ASCAP)
see Walt Disney Music

Burthen Music Co., Inc. (ASCAP)
see Chappell & Co., Inc.

Buttnugget Publishing (ASCAP)
207 1/2 1st Ave. S.
Seattle, Washington 98104

C

C. Israel Music (ASCAP)
see Warner-Chappell Music

Caliv Music (ASCAP)
see Universal-MCA Music Publishing

Camad Music, Inc. (BMI)
c/o Curtom Publishing Co., Inc.
5915 N. Lincoln Ave.
Chicago, Illinois 60645

Camex Music Inc. (BMI)
489 5th Ave.
New York, New York 10017

Cancelled Lunch Music (ASCAP)
see Universal-MCA Music Publishing

Canteberry Music (BMI)
see Warner-Chappell Music

Cappagh Hill Music (BMI)
see EMI Music Publishing

Carbert Music Inc. (BMI)
1619 Broadway, Rm. 609
New York, New York 10019

Careers-BMG Music
see BMG Music

Caroljac Music (BMI)
see Mighty Nice Music

Celedia Music (BMI)
see Warner-Chappell Music

Chante 7 Music (BMI)
see EMI Music Publishing

Chappell & Co., Inc. (ASCAP)
see Warner-Chappell Music

Charm Trap Music (BMI)
see EMI Music Publishing

Chase Chad Music (ASCAP)
see EMI Music Publishing

Cherry Lane Music Co. (ASCAP)
6 E. 32nd St., 11th Fl.
New York, New York 10016

Cherry River Music Co. (BMI)
see Cherry Lane Music Co.

Chi-Boy (ASCAP)
c/o Schwartz & Farquharson
9107 Wilshire Blvd., Ste. 300
Beverly Hills, California 90216

Children of the Forest Music (BMI)
see EMI Music Publishing

Chrysalis Music Group (ASCAP)
Attn: Jeff Brabec
8500 Melrose, 2nd Fl.
Los Angeles, California 90069

Chubby Music (ASCAP)
see Famous Music Corp.

Chyna Baby Music (BMI)
see EMI Music Publishing

Civis Rex Music (ASCAP)
see Warner-Chappell Music

CMI America (ASCAP)
1102 17th Ave. S.
Nashville, Tennessee 37212

Code Word Nemesis (ASCAP)
120 NE State St., No. 418
Olympia, Washington 98501

George M. Cohan Music Publishing Co.
(ASCAP)
c/o Freddy Bienstock Enterprises
1619 Broadway
New York, New York 10019

Colden Grey Music (ASCAP)
Grubman, Indursky, Schindler & Gold
152 W. 57th St.
New York, New York 10019

Colgems-EMI Music (ASCAP)
see EMI Music Publishing

Colonel Rebel Music (ASCAP)
see Magnolia Hill Music

Colpix (BMI)
see Sony ATV Music

Colter Bay Music (BMI)
see Almo Music Corp.

Columbine Music Inc. (ASCAP)
see United Artists Music Co., Inc.

Janice Combs Music (ASCAP)
see EMI Music Publishing

Justin Combs Music (ASCAP)
see EMI Music Publishing

Come on In Music (ASCAP)
see Bro N' Sis Music

Commander Music (ASCAP)
c/o 20th Century Music
10585 Santa Monica Blvd.
Los Angeles, California 90025

Commando Brabdo Music (ASCAP)
see Hitco Music

Connotation Music (BMI)
see Warner-Chappell Music

Constant Pressure Music (BMI)
see Warner-Chappell Music

Controversy Music (ASCAP)
c/o Ziffren Brittenham & Branca
2121 Ave. of the Stars
Los Angeles, California 90067

Conversation Tree Music (ASCAP)
see Zomba Music

Cooltonic Music (ASCAP)
see Famous Music Corp.

Cootermo Music (ASCAP)
418 E. Thompson Ln.
Nashville, Tennessee 37211

Copyright Control
Address Unavailable

Cord Kayla Music (ASCAP)
see EMI Music Publishing

Cori Tiffani Music (BMI)
see Warner-Chappell Music

Corner of Clark and Kent (BMI)
see EMI Music Publishing

Cradle the Balls Music (ASCAP)
see Warner-Chappell Music

Robert Cray Music (BMI)
c/o Rosebud Agency
Box 170429
San Francisco, California 94117

Crazy Crow Music (BMI)
see Siquomb Publishing Corp.

Crazy Owl Music (BMI)
see EMI Music Publishing

List of Publishers

Creeping Death Music (ASCAP)
c/o Manatt Phelps Rothenberg & Tunney
11355 W. Olympic Blvd.
Los Angeles, California 90064

Cristjen Music (BMI)
see Warner-Chappell Music

Crited Music (BMI)
see Warner-Chappell Music

Cross Town Music (BMI)
Address Unavailable

Mike Curb Productions (BMI)
948 Tourmaline Dr.
Newbury Park, California 91220

Cyanide Breathmint Music (ASCAP)
see BMG Music

Cyptron Music (BMI)
see EMI Music Publishing

D

Dakoda House Music (ASCAP)
see EMI Music Publishing

D&W Tone Music (ASCAP)
see Trans Continental Music

Leshawn Daniels (BMI)
see EMI Music Publishing

DCLXVL Music (BMI)
see Dinger & Ollie Music

Dead Game Music (ASCAP)
see Warner-Chappell Music

Dead Solid Perfect Music (BMI)
see Sony ATV Music

Deep Fork Music, Inc. (ASCAP)
15 E. 48th St.
New York, New York 10017

Demis Music (ASCAP)
see EMI Music Publishing

Demolition Man Music (BMI)
see Put It Down Music

Demontes Music (BMI)
see Universal-MCA Music Publishing

Denonation Music (SESAC)
see Warner-Chappell Music

Designa Music (BMI)
see Almo/Irving Music

Desmophobia (ASCAP)
see Polygram Music Publishing Inc.

Dick Johnson Music (ASCAP)
Address Unavailable

Dinger & Ollie Music (BMI)
see Duke T

Walt Disney Music (ASCAP)
500 S. Buena Vista St.
Burbank, California 91521

Divided (BMI)
see Zomba House

Dixie Stars Music (ASCAP)
see Hori Pro Entertainment Group

DJ Irv (BMI)
see EMI Music Publishing

Do What I Gotta Music (ASCAP)
see EMI Music Publishing

Dog Dream (ASCAP)
Box 483
Newton Centre, Massachusetts 02159

Dotted Line Music (ASCAP)
see Zomba Music

Dreamin' Upstream Music (ASCAP)
see Warner-Chappell Music

Dreamworks (BMI)
Address Unavailable

Dub's World Music (ASCAP)
see MCA Music

Duchess Music Corp. (BMI)
1755 Broadway, 8th Fl.
New York, New York 10019

Duke T (BMI)
11355 W. Olympic Blvd.
Los Angeles, California 90064

Dulaney House Music (BMI)
see Famous Music Corp.

Michael Dulaney Music (BMI)
see Famous Music Corp.

Dyad Music, Ltd. (BMI)
c/o Mason & Co.
400 Park Ave.
New York, New York 10022

E

E Equals Music (BMI)
see Warner-Chappell Music

E-Forty Music (BMI)
see Zomba Music

Ecaf Music (BMI)
see Sony ATV Music

Eddie F. Music (ASCAP)
see Warner-Chappell Music

Emancipated Music (ASCAP)
Address Unavailable

EMI-April Music (ASCAP)
see EMI Music Publishing

EMI-Blackwood Music Inc. (BMI)
see EMI Music Publishing

EMI-Full Keel Music (ASCAP)
see EMI Music Publishing

EMI Hastings Music (ASCAP)
see EMI Music Publishing

EMI Music Publishing
1290 Avenue of the Americas
New York, New York 10104

EMI Solvang Music (BMI)
see EMI Music Publishing

EMI-Songs of Windswept Pacific (BMI)
see EMI Music Publishing

EMI Tower Street Music (BMI)
see EMI Music Publishing

EMI U Catalogue (ASCAP)
see EMI Music Publishing

EMI Unart Music (BMI)
see EMI Music Publishing

EMI-Virgin (ASCAP)
see EMI Music Publishing

Encore Entertainment (BMI)
see We Make Music

Endless Soft Hits Music (BMI)
see BMG Music

Englishtown Music (BMI)
see EMI Music Publishing

Seamus Ennis Music (BMI)
see Sony ATV Music

Ensign Music (BMI)
see Famous Music Corp.

Essex Music International (ASCAP)
see EMI Music Publishing

Estefan Music (ASCAP)
see Foreign Imported

Estes Park Music (BMI)
see Bro N' Sis Music

EZ Music (ASCAP)
see Sony ATV Music

F

Family Style Music (SESAC)
see EMI Music Publishing

Famous Music Corp. (ASCAP)
  10635 Santa Monica Blvd.
  Ste. 300
  Los Angeles, California 90025

FHW Music (ASCAP)
  8900 Wilshire Blvd., Ste.300
  Beverly Hills, California 90211

Fiddleback (BMI)
  see Valando Group

Fire Feather Music (ASCAP)
  see Mighty Nice Music

Fleetside Music (BMI)
  see CMI America

Floyd's Dream Music (ASCAP)
  see BMG Music

Flying Earform (BMI)
  see EMI Music Publishing

Flyte Tyme Tunes (ASCAP)
  c/o Margo Matthews
  Box 92004
  Los Angeles, California 90009

Follazoo Music (ASCAP)
  see We Make Music

Foreign Imported (BMI)
  8921 S.W. Tenth Terrace
  Miami, Florida 33174

Fort Knox Music Co. (BMI)
  1619 Broadway, 11th Fl.
  New York, New York 10019

Ft. Toe Music (BMI)
  see Bug Music

4MW Music (ASCAP)
  see Zomba Music

Fourth Floor Music Inc. (ASCAP)
  Wirrenberg Rd., Rte. 212
  Bearsville, New York 12409

Fox Film Music Corp. (BMI)
  c/o Twentieth Century Fox Film Corp
  PO Box 900
  Beverly Hills, California 90213

Len Freedman Music
  123 El Paseo
  Santa Barbara, California 93101

Fresh Avery Music (BMI)
  see Sony ATV Music

Frontera Music (ASCAP)
  Box 3020
  Canutillo, Texas 79835

Dwight Frye (BMI)
  Address Unavailable

Fun with Goats Music (ASCAP)
  see EMI Music Publishing

Future Furniture Music (ASCAP)
  see Screen Gems-EMI Music Inc.

G

Al Gallico Music Corp. (BMI)
  9301 Wilshire, Ste. 311
  Beverly Hills, California 90210

Michael Garvin Music (BMI)
  see Warner-Chappell Music

Genevieve Music (ASCAP)
  c/o Wixen Music Publishing Inc.
  PO Box 260317
  Encino, California 91426

Gifted Source Music (ASCAP)
  47 E. Queensway, Ste. 207
  Hampton, Virginia 23669

Glacier Park Music (SESAC)
  see EMI Music Publishing

Gladys Music (ASCAP)
  see Hudson Bay Music

Gnat Booty Music (ASCAP)
  see Camex Music Inc.

Golden Mountain Music Inc. (ASCAP)
  c/o Freedman Snow & Co.
  1092 Mount Pleasant Rd.
  Toronto, Ontario M4P 2M6
  Canada

Golden Wheat Music (BMI)
  see Warner-Chappell Music

Good Ol Delta Boys Music (SESAC)
  Box 9287
  Jackson, Mississippi 39286

Gracey Rhodes Prod. (ASCAP)
  see Almo/Irving Music

Gramily Music (ASCAP)
  see Peer Music

Grantsville (ASCAP)
  see Zomba Music

Grave Lack of Talent Music (BMI)
  see Warner-Chappell Music

Griff Griff Music (ASCAP)
  see Warner-Chappell Music

Groin Pull Music (ASCAP)
  see Womanly Hips Music

Groove Child Music (BMI)
  see Universal-MCA Music Publishing

Grosse Point Harlem Music (BMI)
  see Future Furniture Music

Grung Girl Music (ASCAP)
  see EMI Music Publishing

Guns N' Roses Music (ASCAP)
  c/o Prager and Fenton
  1324 Wilshire Blvd.
  Los Angeles, California 90025

H

Hamstein Cumberland (BMI)
  1033 18th Ave. S.
  Nashville, Tennessee 37212

Happenstance Music
  Address Unavailable

Happy Ditties from Paradise (ASCAP)
  see EMI Music Publishing

Heavenly Sounds Music (BMI)
  see Warner-Chappell Music

Hee Bee Doinit (ASCAP)
  see EMI Music Publishing

Hellmaymen (BMI)
  see Warner-Chappell Music

Herbilicious Music (ASCAP)
  see Warner-Chappell Music

Hidden Pun Music (BMI)
  1841 Broadway
  New York, New York 10023

Hit Co. South (ASCAP)
  see Sony ATV Music

Hitco Music (BMI)
  see Warner-Chappell Music

Honey from Missouri Music (ASCAP)
  see Famous Music Corp.

Hope Chest Music (BMI)
  see Universal-MCA Music Publishing

Hori Pro Entertainment Group (ASCAP)
  1819 Broadway
  Nashville, Tennessee 37203

House of Bryant Publications (BMI)
  PO Box 570
  Gatlinburg, Tennessee 37738

House of Integrity Music (BMI)
  see Warner-Chappell Music

Hub Music (ASCAP)
  see Commander Music

Hudson Bay Music (BMI)
  1619 Broadway
  New York, New York 10019

Huss-Zwingli Music (ASCAP)
see Sony ATV Music

I

I Like Em Thicke Music (ASCAP)
see EMI Music Publishing

If Dreams Had Wings (ASCAP)
c/o CMRRA
56 Wellesley St., W.
Toronto, Ontario M5S 2S4
Canada

India B Music (BMI)
see Universal-MCA Music Publishing

Innocent Criminal (ASCAP)
see EMI Music Publishing

Irving Music Inc. (BMI)
360 N. LaCienega Blvd.
Los Angeles, California 90048

Island Music (BMI)
6525 Sunset Blvd.
Los Angeles, California 90028

Itall Shur Music (ASCAP)
see Sony ATV Music

Itchy Putschy (BMI)
see Warner-Chappell Music

J

J. Fred Knoblock Music (ASCAP)
see Lebrun Ingram Music

Jacksnacks Music (ASCAP)
see Womanly Hips Music

Jagermeister Music (ASCAP)
see EMI Music Publishing

Jalma Music (ASCAP)
see Island Music

Jaywood Music (BMI)
see EMI Music Publishing

Jazz Merchant Music (ASCAP)
see Zomba Music

Jelly's Jams L.L.C. Music (BMI)
see EMI Music Publishing

Jerk Awake Music (ASCAP)
c/o Manatt Phelps & Phillips
11355 W. Olympic Blvd.
Los Angeles, California 90064

Rodney Jerkins Music (BMI)
see EMI Music Publishing

Fred Jerkins Publishing (BMI)
see EMI Music Publishing

Jermaine Music (ASCAP)
see Sony ATV Music

Jezebel Blues Music (BMI)
Address Unavailable

Jimi-Lane Music (BMI)
PO Box 5295, Ocean Park Sta.
Santa Monica, California 90405

Jobete Music Co. (ASCAP)
see EMI Music Publishing

Jondora Music (BMI)
Tenth & Parker St.s
Berkeley, California 94710

Jones Fall Music (BMI)
see EMI Music Publishing

Jones Music America (ASCAP)
c/o Dorothy Mae Rice Jones
416 W. 9th St., No. 1312
Cincinnati, Ohio 45203

Hudson Jordan (ASCAP)
see Wixen Music

Steven A. Jordan Music (ASCAP)
see EMI Music Publishing

Josma's Dream Music (BMI)
see Universal-MCA Music Publishing

Jumping Bean Music (ASCAP)
see EMI Music Publishing

Jungle Fever Music (BMI)
   see Almo/Irving Music

K

Kababa Music (ASCAP)
   c/o Pen Music Group
   6255 Sunset Blvd., Ste. 1024
   Los Angeles, California 90028-7407

Kalinmia (ASCAP)
   see EMI Music Publishing

Kandacy Music (ASCAP)
   see EMI Music Publishing

Kander & Ebb Inc. (BMI)
   see Valando Group

Kar Tay Music
   Address Unavailable

Karima Music (BMI)
   see Warner-Chappell Music

Blake Karrington Music (BMI)
   see EMI Music Publishing

Keily Music (ASCAP)
   see Zomba Music

Kelendria Music (ASCAP)
   see EMI Music Publishing

R. Kelly Music (BMI)
   see Zomba Music

Kent Greene Music (BMI)
   see Sony ATV Music

Kentucky Thunder Music (ASCAP)
   see Magnolia Hill Music

Kharatroy Music (ASCAP)
   see Chrysalis Music Group

Kid Capri (ASCAP)
   see EMI Music Publishing

Kinetic Diamond Music (ASCAP)
   513 Hill Rd.
   Nashville, Tennessee 37220

Stephen A. Kipner Music (ASCAP)
   Attn: Stephen A. Kipner
   19646 Valley View Dr.
   Topanga, California 90290

Jordan Knight Music (ASCAP)
   see EMI Music Publishing

Koh Music (ASCAP)
   see Chrysalis Music Group

L

Lady Diamond Music (BMI)
   see Universal-MCA Music Publishing

Laudersongs (BMI)
   see Mighty Nice Music

B.K. Lawrence Music (BMI)
   see Warner-Chappell Music

Le Tonya Music (ASCAP)
   see EMI Music Publishing

Leaning Tower Music (BMI)
   see EMI Music Publishing

Leaving Hope Music (ASCAP)
   see TVT

Lebrun Ingram Music (ASCAP)
   c/o Louis Spoctore
   1201 16th Ave. S.
   Nashville, Tennessee 37212

Lehsem Music (BMI)
   see EMI Music Publishing

Jerry Leiber Music (ASCAP)
   9000 Sunset Blvd.
   Ste. 1107
   Los Angeles, California 90069

Levar's Cribb Music (ASCAP)
   see Famous Music Corp.

Light Gyrl Music (ASCAP)
   see Almo/Irving Music

Lil Lu Lu Music (BMI)
   see EMI Music Publishing

Lil Mob Music (ASCAP)
see EMI Music Publishing

Jinsoo Lim Music (ASCAP)
see EMI Music Publishing

Line On Music (ASCAP)
see EMI Music Publishing

Lit Up Music (ASCAP)
see Famous Music Corp.

Little B (ASCAP)
see EMI Music Publishing

Little Cayman (BMI)
see EMI Music Publishing

Little Idiot Music (BMI)
see Warner-Chappell Music

Little Tomatoes Music (BMI)
see Warner-Chappell Music

Living Under a Rock Music (BMI)
see EMI Music Publishing

Llewes Music (BMI)
220 Cumberland St., Apt. 2R
Brooklyn, New York 11205

Lo Giene Music (BMI)
see EMI Music Publishing

Loco De Amor (BMI)
1775 Broadway
New York, New York 10019

Logo Music
see BMG Music

Loobiecore Music
Address Unavailable

Loon Echo Music (BMI)
see Zomba Music

Love N Loyalty Music (BMI)
see EMI Music Publishing

Love Ranch Music (ASCAP)
see EMI Music Publishing

Lovely Sorts of Death Music (BMI)
see EMI Music Publishing

Lowery Music Co., Inc. (BMI)
3051 Clairmont Rd., N.E.
Atlanta, Georgia 30329

Lucky Ladybug Music (BMI)
see Reynsong Music

Lungclam Music (ASCAP)
see Buttnugget Publishing

M

Mack Loyd Wadkins Music (ASCAP)
see Boondocks Music

Mad Dog Winston Music (BMI)
see Warner-Chappell Music

Magnature Music (SESAC)
see EMI Music Publishing

Magnetic Music Publishing Co. (ASCAP)
5 Jones St., Apt. 4
New York, New York 10014

Magnolia Hill Music (BMI)
Box 50
Nashville, Tennessee 37202

Major Bob Music (ASCAP)
1109 17th Ave. S
Nashville, Tennessee 37212

Malaco Music Co. (BMI)
PO Box 9287
Jackson, Mississippi 39206

Mammy's Geetar Music (BMI)
86 Tuttle Rd.
Cumberland, Maine 04021

Aimee Mann
see You Can't Take It With You

Manuiti LA Music (ASCAP)
see Warner-Chappell Music

Marshall Music (ASCAP)
see EMI Music Publishing

Mason Betha Music (ASCAP)
see EMI Music Publishing

Mass Confusion Music (ASCAP)
see Warner-Chappell Music

Matragun Music Inc. (BMI)
c/o Jess S. Morgan & Co.
6420 Wilshire Blvd., 19th Fl.
Los Angeles, California 90048

Matt Music (BMI)
see Universal-MCA Music Publishing

Mawkeens Music (ASCAP)
see Sony ATV Music

MCA, Inc. (ASCAP)
see Universal-MCA Music Publishing

MCA Music (ASCAP)
see Universal-MCA Music Publishing

McSpadden-Smith Music (ASCAP)
see Magnolia Hill Music

Meg Alex Music (BMI)
see Warner-Chappell Music

Mel Boopie Music (BMI)
see EMI Music Publishing

Melusic Music (ASCAP)
see EMI Music Publishing

Tony Mercedes Music (ASCAP)
see EMI Music Publishing

Metcom Music
Address Unavailable

Mighty Nice Music (BMI)
see Polygram Music Publishing Inc.

Miller Music Corp. (ASCAP)
see United Artists Music Co., Inc.

Mills Music Inc. (ASCAP)
see EMI Music Publishing

Mint Condition Music (ASCAP)
see EMI Music Publishing

Mississippi Mud Music (BMI)
see Warner-Chappell Music

Miti Music (SESAC)
see Universal-MCA Music Publishing

MJ12 Music (BMI)
see EMI Music Publishing

MLE Music (ASCAP)
see Almo Music Corp.

Mo Better Grooves Music (ASCAP)
see Famous Music Corp.

Mo Fuzzy Dice Music (ASCAP)
see Famous Music Corp.

Moebetoblame Music (BMI)
1990 Bundy Dr.
Los Angeles, California 90025

Money Mack Music (BMI)
Address Unavailable

Money Man Music (ASCAP)
see Famous Music Corp.

Monkey Demon Music (BMI)
see EMI Music Publishing

Moraine (BMI)
see Famous Music Corp.

Morley Music Co., Inc. (ASCAP)
c/o Eastman & Eastman
39 W. 54th St.
New York, New York 10019

Edwin H. Morris
see MPL Communications Inc.

Moseka Music (ASCAP)
940 St. Nicholas Ave.
Apt. 5E
New York, New York 10032

Motown Songs (BMI)
see Universal-MCA Music Publishing

MPL Communications Inc. (ASCAP)
c/o Lee Eastman
39 W. 54th St.
New York, New York 10019

Mr. Bubba Music (BMI)
see Sony ATV Music

Mr. Noise Music (BMI)
see We Make Music

MRI Music (ASCAP)
see EMI Music Publishing

Muffin Stuffin (BMI)
3624 Fir
San Diego, California 92104

Music City Music (ASCAP)
see EMI Music Publishing

Music Hill Music (BMI)
54 Music Sq. E., Ste. 202
Nashville, Tennessee 37203

Music by Nickelodean (ASCAP)
see EMI Music Publishing

Music Sales Corp. (ASCAP)
257 Park Ave. S., 20th Fl.
New York, New York 10010

My Life's Work Music (ASCAP)
see EMI Music Publishing

My So Called Music (ASCAP)
7307 Crowne Brook Circle
Franklin, Tennessee 37067

Myrt & Chuck's Boy Music (ASCAP)
see Cootermo Music

N

Naked Under My Clothes Music (ASCAP)
see Warner-Chappell Music

Neon Sky Music (ASCAP)
see EMI Music Publishing

New Haven Music (BMI)
see PolyGram Records Inc.

New Works Music (BMI)
see Warner-Chappell Music

Randy Newman Music (ASCAP)
c/o Gelfand, Rennert & Feldman
1880 Century Park, E., Ste. 900
Los Angeles, California 90067

19 Music
Address Unavailable

Nomad-Noman Music (BMI)
see Warner-Chappell Music

Noontime Music (ASCAP)
see Chrysalis Music Group

Norick Music
144 Broad Ave.
Leona, New Jersey 07606

Notable Music Co., Inc. (ASCAP)
Cy Coleman Enterprises
200 W. 54th St.
New York, New York 10019

Nuyorican Publishing (BMI)
see Sony ATV Music

O

O' Brook Music (BMI)
see EMI Music Publishing

Obverse Creation Music (ASCAP)
see Sony ATV Music

October 12th Music (ASCAP)
see Universal-MCA Music Publishing

Oh God Music (ASCAP)
see Universal-MCA Music Publishing

Old Crow (BMI)
10585 Santa Monica Blvd.
Los Angeles, California 90025

Old Dirty Music (BMI)
see Warner-Chappell Music

Oleander Noise Music (BMI)
see Universal-MCA Music Publishing

Only Hit Music (BMI)
see MCA Music

Orbit Music (BMI)
see EMI Music Publishing

Otherwise (ASCAP)
see Otherwise Publishing

Otherwise Publishing (ASCAP)
c/o Mark Tanner
9595 Wilshire Blvd.
Beverly Hills, California 90212

Owen Pop Music (ASCAP)
see Warner-Chappell Music

P

P-Blast Music (ASCAP)
see Zomba Music

Paradise Ave. Music (BMI)
see Warner-Chappell Music

Paradise Forever Music (BMI)
see Universal-MCA Music Publishing

Partnt Music (ASCAP)
see Acuff Rose Music

PB Music (ASCAP)
c/o David Franklin
1201 Peachtree
Atlanta, Georgia 30309

Peer International Corp. (BMI)
see Peer-Southern Organization

Peer Music (BMI)
see PSO Ltd.

Peer-Southern Organization (ASCAP)
810 7th Ave.
New York, New York 10019

Peermusic Ltd. (BMI)
see Peer-Southern Organization

Pepper Drive Music (BMI)
see EMI Music Publishing

Carl Perkins Music (BMI)
see Warner-Chappell Music

A Phantom Vox Music (BMI)
see Warner-Chappell Music

Pink Jeans Music (SESAC)
see Zomba Music

PLX Music (ASCAP)
see Famous Music Corp.

Plyner Music
Address Unavailable

Poet Tree Music (ASCAP)
see Blackhawk Music Co.

Poeyfarre Music (BMI)
see Bug Music

Pogo Stick Music (BMI)
see Brentwood Music

Polygram International Music (ASCAP)
see Universal-MCA Music Publishing

Polygram Music Publishing Inc. (ASCAP)
see Universal-MCA Music Publishing

PolyGram Records Inc. (ASCAP)
see Universal-MCA Music Publishing

Elvis Presley Music (BMI)
see Warner-Chappell Music

Hugh Prestwood (BMI)
see BMG Music

Price is Right Music (ASCAP)
see MCA Music

Proudfoot Music (BMI)
see Stay Straight Music

PSO Ltd. (ASCAP)
see Peer-Southern Organization

Puddy Tat Music (BMI)
see Universal-MCA Music Publishing

Purple Crayon Music (ASCAP)
see Sony ATV Music

List of Publishers

Put It Down Music (SESAC)
11440 Ventura Blvd., Ste. 200
Studio City, California 91604

Q

Quality First Music (ASCAP)
see Warner-Chappell Music

Queen Music Ltd. (BMI)
see EMI Music Publishing

R

Rahzel Music (BMI)
see Universal-MCA Music Publishing

Raje Music (BMI)
see Warner-Chappell Music

Rassmysteria Music (ASCAP)
see Warner-Chappell Music

Realsongs (ASCAP)
Attn: Diane Warren
6363 Sunset Blvd., Ste. 810
Hollywood, California 90028

Red Brazos (BMI)
Box 163870
Austin, Texas 78716

Retribution Music (BMI)
see Sony ATV Music

Revolutionary Jazz Giant (BMI)
see Warner-Chappell Music

Reynsong Music (BMI)
215 E. Wentworth Ave.
West St. Paul, Minnesota 55118

Riddim Kingdom Music (BMI)
see Zomba Music

Right Bank Music
see Warner-Chappell Music

Righteous Babe Music (BMI)
P. O. Box 95, Ellicott Station
Buffalo, New York 14205

Rive Droite Music (BMI)
c/o Haber Corp.
16830 Ventura Blvd., Ste. 501
Encino, California 91436

Roastitoasti Music (ASCAP)
see EMI Music Publishing

Rob 'N Riley Music (ASCAP)
see Peer Music

Robert Hill Music (BMI)
see Warner-Chappell Music

Toni Robi Music (ASCAP)
see 2000 Watts Music

Rondor Music Inc. (ASCAP)
see Almo Music Corp.

Rough Cut Music (BMI)
see EMI Music Publishing

The Phil Roy Music (ASCAP)
see Warner-Chappell Music

RPM Music (ASCAP)
see Warner-Chappell Music

R.S.O. Publishing Inc. (ASCAP)
see Chappell & Co., Inc.

RTP Music (BMI)
182 Eastwood Drive
Aspen, Colorado 81611

Rufftown Music (BMI)
see Famous Music Corp.

Rushing Water Music (ASCAP)
see Magnolia Hill Music

Rusty Knuckles Music (BMI)
see Warner-Chappell Music

Rye Songs (BMI)
see Sony ATV Music

S

Safe Cracker Music (ASCAP)
see Hitco Music

Sailmaker Music (ASCAP)
Attn: Robert M. Millsap
PO Box 1028
Hot Springs, Arizona 71902

St. Julien Music (ASCAP)
see Universal-MCA Music Publishing

A Salt on the Charts Music (ASCAP)
see Zomba Music

Sang Melee Music (BMI)
see Warner-Chappell Music

Boz Scaggs Music (ASCAP)
c/o Front Line Management
9044 Melrose Ave., 3rd Fl.
Los Angeles, California 90069

Scott & Soda Music (ASCAP)
see Sony ATV Music

Screen Gems-EMI Music Inc. (BMI)
6255 Sunset Blvd., 12th Fl.
Hollywood, California 90028

Scrogrow Music (BMI)
see Warner-Chappell Music

Sea Bayle Music (ASCAP)
see EMI Music Publishing

See No Evil Music (ASCAP)
c/o Ronda Espy
Box 8649
Universal City, California 91618

See Squared Music (BMI)
see Warner-Chappell Music

Sell the Cow Music (BMI)
see Warner-Chappell Music

Seven Music (BMI)
200 W. 51st St.
New York, New York 10019

Shapiro, Bernstein & Co., Inc. (ASCAP)
Attn: Leon Brettler
640 5th Ave.
New York, New York 10019

Shek' Em Down Music (BMI)
see Hitco Music

Shep Shep Music (ASCAP)
see Famous Music Corp.

Shillelagh Music (BMI)
see EMI Music Publishing

Shobi Music (BMI)
c/o DeBarris Music
1107 17th Ave. S.
Nashville, Tennessee 37212

Silkie Music (BMI)
see Universal-MCA Music Publishing

Silver Fiddle (ASCAP)
c/o Segel & Goldman Inc.
9200 Sunset Blvd., Ste. 1000
Los Angeles, California 90069

Silverkiss Music (BMI)
see Warner-Chappell Music

Siquomb Publishing Corp. (BMI)
c/o Segel & Goldman Inc.
9348 Santa Monica Blvd.
Beverly Hills, California 90210

Sixteen Stars Music (BMI)
see Dixie Stars Music

Sixty Four Square Music
Address Unavailable

Sky Music
Address Unavailable

Slack A. D. Music (ASCAP)
see EMI Music Publishing

Slam U Well Music (BMI)
see Warner-Chappell Music

Sleez Tak Music (ASCAP)
see Womanly Hips Music

Smash Vegas (ASCAP)
see EMI Music Publishing

Smith Haven Music (ASCAP)
see Warner-Chappell Music

Arlos Smith Music (SESAC)
see Good Ol Delta Boys Music

SMY Music (ASCAP)
see EMI Music Publishing

Snowden Music (ASCAP)
Box 11512th St.
Purdys, New York 10578

So Do My Songs (ASCAP)
Detour M, Box 491
New York, New York 10101

Song of Peer (BMI)
see Peer International Corp.

Songs of Golgotha (BMI)
see Dinger & Ollie Music

Songs of Nashville (BMI)
see Warner-Chappell Music

Songs of Polygram (BMI)
see Polygram International Music

Songs of Universal (BMI)
see Universal-MCA Music Publishing

Sony ATV Cross Keys Publishing Co. Inc.
c/o Donna Hilley
PO Box 1273
Nashville, Tennessee 37202

Sony ATV Music (ASCAP)
550 Madison Ave.
New York, New York 10022

Sony ATV Songs (BMI)
see Sony ATV Music

Sony ATV Tree Publishing (BMI)
1111 16th Ave. S.
Nashville, Tennessee 37212

Southern Days Music (ASCAP)
see EMI Music Publishing

Sovereign Music Corp. (ASCAP)
c/o Al Lewis
22 E. 49th St.
New York, New York 10017

Sparrow Song Music (BMI)
Box 5085
Brentwood, Tennessee 37204

Special Rider Music (SESAC)
PO Box 860, Cooper Sta.
New York, New York 10276

Sporty Music (ASCAP)
see Hitco Music

Mark Alan Springer Music (BMI)
see EMI Music Publishing

Bruce Springsteen Publishing (ASCAP)
c/o Jon Landau Management, Inc.
Attn: Barbara Carr
136 E. 57th St., No. 1202
New York, New York 10021

Squamosal Music (BMI)
see Warner-Chappell Music

Squish Moth Music (ASCAP)
see Warner-Chappell Music

Allen Stanton Productions (ASCAP)
see Jerry Leiber Music

Stapp/Tremonti Music (BMI)
c/o Wind Up Records
72 Madison Ave.
New York, New York 10016

Starstruck Writers Group (ASCAP)
PO Box 121996
Nashville, Tennessee 37212

Stay Straight Music (BMI)
c/o E.G. Music
9157 Sunset Blvd.
Los Angeles, California 90069

Steel Burg Music (ASCAP)
see Hitco Music

Stellabella Music (BMI)
see Colden Grey Music

Still Working for the Man Music (BMI)
see Sony ATV Music

Mike Stoller Music (ASCAP)
9000 Sunset Blvd.
Ste. 1107
Los Angeles, California 90069

Storm King Music Inc. (BMI)
250 W. 57th St., Ste. 2017
New York, New York 10019

Streamline Moderne (BMI)
see Warner-Chappell Music

Studio Nomado Music (BMI)
see Sony ATV Music

Sugar Bend Music (BMI)
see Warner-Chappell Music

Sugar Free Music
Address Unavailable

Sundance Kid Music (ASCAP)
see Universal-MCA Music Publishing

Sushi Too Music (BMI)
see Warner-Chappell Music

Sweet Woo Music (SESAC)
see Warner-Chappell Music

Swizz Beats Music (ASCAP)
see Warner-Chappell Music

Sword and Stone Music (ASCAP)
10209 Gary Rd.
Potomac, Maryland 20854

Keith Sykes Music (BMI)
c/o Keith Sykes
3974 Hawkins Mill Rd.
Memphis, Tennessee 38128

T

T-Boy Music Publishing Co., Inc. (ASCAP)
c/o Lipservices
1841 Broadway
New York, New York 10023

T. Scott Style Music (SESAC)
see Put It Down Music

Tabulous Music (ASCAP)
see Famous Music Corp.

Tallest Tree Music (ASCAP)
see Polygram Music Publishing Inc.

Tam Music (BMI)
see Hitco Music

Tay Kar Music
Address Unavailable

TCF Music (ASCAP)
see Warner-Chappell Music

Te Bass (BMI)
see EMI Music Publishing

Temporary Music (BMI)
see Warner-Chappell Music

Tender Tunes Music Co., Inc. (BMI)
c/o Werner Hintzen
United Artists Music Co., Inc.
6753 Hollywood Blvd.
Los Angeles, California 90028

Thelma's Boi Music (BMI)
see Universal-MCA Music Publishing

Them Damn Twins Music (ASCAP)
see Chrysalis Music Group

Thirtytwo Mile Music (BMI)
see Warner-Chappell Music

3EB Music (BMI)
see EMI Music Publishing

Tickson Music (BMI)
see Len Freedman Music

Timon Music (BMI)
see EMI Music Publishing

To the Third Power Music (BMI)
see EMI Music Publishing

Tobaki Music (ASCAP)
see Famous Music Corp.

Tosha Music (ASCAP)
see EMI Music Publishing

List of Publishers

Tranquility Base Songs (ASCAP)
see Warner-Chappell Music

Trans Continental Music (ASCAP)
Address Unavailable

Traveling Zoo (ASCAP)
see Beginner Music

Treat Baker Music (SOCAN)
c/o NGB Inc.
579 Richmond St. W., Ste. 401
Toronto, Ontario M5V1Y6
Canada

Treble Kicker Music (BMI)
see EMI Music Publishing

Treyball Music (ASCAP)
see Sony ATV Music

Tricky Track Music (BMI)
113 Abbottsford Gate
Piermont, New York 10968

Trio Music Co., Inc. (BMI)
c/o Leiber & Stoller
9000 Sunset Blvd., Ste. 1107
Los Angeles, California 90069

Tunes by Nickelodean (BMI)
see EMI Music Publishing

Tunes on the Verge of Insanity (BMI)
see Famous Music Corp.

TVT (ASCAP)
23 E. 4th St.
NYC, New York 10003

Twelve & Under Music (ASCAP)
see EMI Music Publishing

Twentieth Century-Fox Music Corp. (ASCAP)
Attn: Herbert N. Eiseman
PO Box 900
Beverly Hills, California 90213

27th and May Music (ASCAP)
see EMI Music Publishing

Twisted Music (ASCAP)
see EMI Music Publishing

2000 Watts Music (ASCAP)
c/o Darrell Allanby
375 Mt. Prospect Ave.
Newark, New Jersey 07104

Tyde (BMI)
see Sony ATV Music

Tyland Music (BMI)
see EMI Music Publishing

T'Ziah's Music (BMI)
see EMI Music Publishing

U

Uncle Ivan Music (BMI)
Box 730
Franklin, Tennessee 37065

Unconcerned Music (BMI)
see EMI Music Publishing

Underachiever Music (BMI)
23564 Calabasas Rd., Ste. 107
Calabasas, California 91302

Unichappell Music Inc. (BMI)
see Warner-Chappell Music

United Artists Music Co., Inc.
6753 Hollywood Blvd.
Los Angeles, California 90028

United Lion Music Inc. (BMI)
c/o United Artists Corp.
729 7th Ave.
New York, New York 10019

Universal-MCA Music Publishing (ASCAP)
2440 Sepulveda Blvd., Ste. 100
Los Angeles, California 90064

Universal Music (ASCAP)
see Universal-MCA Music Publishing

Universal Music Corp. (ASCAP)
732 Broadway
New York, New York 10003

Upward Dog Music (ASCAP)
3557 Centinela Ave.
Los Angeles, California 90066

V

Valando Group (BMI)
1233 Avenue of the Americas
New York, New York 10036

Variety Music Inc. (BMI)
c/o Metro-Goldwyn-Mayer, Inc.
10202 W. Washington Blvd.
Culver City, California 90230

Phil Vassar (ASCAP)
see EMI Music Publishing

Vibe Crusher Music (BMI)
see Almo/Irving

Vinny Mae Music (BMI)
50 West Main
Ventura, California 93001

Virgin Music (ASCAP)
see EMI Music Publishing

Virginia Beach Music (ASCAP)
see Warner-Chappell Music

W

Wait and See Music (BMI)
see Warner-Chappell Music

Wajoma Music (BMI)
see Tickson Music

Steve Wariner (BMI)
c/o Siren Songs
Gelfand, Rennert & Feldman
1880 Century Park, E., No. 900
Los Angeles, California 90067

Warner-Chappell Music (ASCAP)
10585 Santa Monica Blvd.
Los Angeles, California 90025

Warner-Tamerlane Music (BMI)
see Warner-Chappell Music

Warren G (BMI)
see Sony ATV Music

The Waters of Nazareth Music (BMI)
see EMI Music Publishing

Wayne's World Music (ASCAP)
see Sony ATV Music

Waysong Music (ASCAP)
c/o Wayfield, Inc.
1136 Gateway Lane
Nashville, Tennessee 37220

WB Music (ASCAP)
10585 Santa Monica Blvd.
Los Angeles, California 90025

We Make Music (BMI)
c/o Fred Conley
5581 Hillview
Brentwood, Tennessee 37027

Wenonga Music (BMI)
see Sony ATV Music

Weowna Music
see Bug Music

When Worlds Collide (ASCAP)
326 Panoramic Hwy.
Mill Valley, California 94941

Why Walk (BMI)
Address Unavailable

Wiggly Tooth Music (ASCAP)
see Warner-Chappell Music

Windswept Pacific (ASCAP)
see EMI Music Publishing

Without Anna Music (ASCAP)
see Magnolia Hill Music

M. Witmark & Sons (ASCAP)
see WB Music

Wixen Music (BMI)
see Warner-Chappell Music

Womanly Hips Music (BMI)
see Polygram Music Publishing Inc.

List of Publishers

Wonderland Music (BMI)
  see Walt Disney Music

Woolly Puddin' Music (BMI)
  see BMG Music

Words Ampersand Music (BMI)
  see Warner-Chappell Music

World Song Publishing, Inc. (ASCAP)
  see Warner-Chappell Music

Wu-Tang Music (BMI)
  see BMG Music

Wunderworld Music (BMI)
  see EMI Music Publishing

Y

Ya Digg Music (ASCAP)
  see EMI Music Publishing

Yah Yah Music (ASCAP)
  see EMI Music Publishing

Yee Haw Music (ASCAP)
  c/o Debbie Doebler
  48 Music Square E.
  Nashville, Tennessee 37203

Yellow Desert Music (BMI)
  see EMI Music Publishing

Yes Dear (BMI)
  see Bug Music

You Can't Take It With You (ASCAP)
  9034 Sunset Blvd., Ste. 250
  Los Angeles, California 90069

You Make Me Sick, I Make Music (ASCAP)
  c/o Manatt Phelps Rothenberg &
  Tunney
  11355 W. Olympic Blvd.
  Los Angeles, California 90064

You Want a Piece of This Music (ASCAP)
  see Bug Music

Young Fiano Music (SESAC)
  see Put It Down Music

Z

Zamalama Music (ASCAP)
  see Good Ol Delta Boys Music

Zomba House (ASCAP)
  137-139 W. 25th St, 8th Floor
  New York, New York 10001

Zomba Music (ASCAP)
  137-139 W. 25th St., 8th Fl.
  New York, New York 10001

ISBN 0-7876-3311-9

90000